UNDERSTA

SUICIDE

LIVING WITH LOSS. PATHS TO PREVENTION.

UNDERSTANDING
SUICIDE
LIVING WITH LOSS. PATHS TO PREVENTION.

PAULA FONTENELLE

UNDERSTANDING SUICIDE

Copyright © 2019 by Paula Fontenelle

First printing, October 2019

Photo cover © Henry Pontual
Model cover: Adriana Duarte Pontual
Cover design: Henry Pontual
Lettering, Illustration, and interior design: Henry Pontual
www.Henrypontual.com

Editor: Dylan Garity

ISBN 978-169150483-1

Paula Fontenelle
www.understandsuicide.com

CONTENTS

Acknowledgements - xi

Prologue - xiii

Introduction - 15

CHAPTER ONE - My story - 25
- Teenage Years
- Adult Life

CHAPTER TWO - What is Suicide? - 77
- Unconscious impulses
- Associated emotions and motivations

CHAPTER THREE - Global Panorama - 87
- Most affected areas
- Global numbers are dropping
- United States, Australia and the United Kingdom
- Gender differences and methods
- Cultural factors
- Other cultural factors

CHAPTER FOUR - Risk Factors - 113
- Previous attempts
- Mental disorders
- Identifying the psychological causes
- Other risk factors
- Protective factors

CHAPTER FIVE - Warning Signs - 139
- Expressing the pain
- Behavioral cues
- What to do
- Additional warning signs

CHAPTER SIX - **Suicide Notes** - 149
- What the letters tell us
- The different types of good-bye

CHAPTER SEVEN - **Those Left Behind** - 161
- What if
- Sadness
- Anger
- Fear of genetic inheritance
- The stigma
- How to tell a child

CHAPTER EIGHT - **How To Treat Suicide Grief: A guide for therapists** - 179
- The popularized phases of grief
- Dr. William Worden's tasks of mourning
- Is suicide bereavement different?
- What makes it unique
- The ever-present stigma
- Suicide within the family context
- Complicated grief
- How families are impacted
- Resilience
- Our bodies as conduits of pain
- Support groups
- Final notes
- Tips from experienced therapists

CHAPTER NINE - **Youth and Suicide: A worldwide concern** - 251
- Social media
- When being online can be deadly
- Rising rates in college students
- Watch for
- What helps
- Self-harm in adolescence
- Non-Suicidal Self-injury (NSSI)
- Other aspects of self-harm

Acknowledgements

People often say that writing a book is a solitary activity. In my experience, this is partly true. In all my books, I have had help from friends and family, from whom I have received valuable ideas, criticism, and suggestions.

I am certain that I could not have finished the new edition of this book without the dedication and support of my sister Renata. I can't even count the number of times I called her frustrated with the bad quality of the translations I received, which meant days of rewriting the material. Not only would she reinforce the importance of having the book in English, but she would redo the translations herself. Many of the chapters were translated by her and she did that in the middle of finishing an undergraduate degree.

Thank you, Renata, for being in my life, and for being who you are.

My dear friend, Gerald, whom I affectionately call "my American dad" also deserves my deep gratitude. For months, he cheered me on, as he has always done, and revised every chapter of this book. Sometimes, after sending me the much-needed corrections, we would have long conversations about the content, the stories I shared, the messages I wanted to convey. With his restless creativity, Gerald would give me ideas for the title, for an angle I hadn't thought of, or simply throw a compliment on a particular chapter or paragraph.

Thank you for all of it.

Henry Pontual, my childhood friend, has professionally touched all my books. He designed my first cover, took the portrait shot used in the second, and created the layout and cover for the third. Not once did I have to ask for his contribution. Real friends do that. They look at you and know what you need, offering their support unconditionally. Again and again, thank you, Rico.

Carolyn Martin, Regina Scharf, and Leslie Storm, I'm deeply grateful for your talent and time revising my writing. Thank you.

Dylan Garity, your meticulous editing immensely improved the quality of this book. Thanks for the dedication and professionalism you showed me.

Finally, without my family's consent and determination to share our story, I would not have been able to begin this journey against the stigma that surrounds suicide. Thank you, mom, Eveline, and Renata for having the courage to expose yourselves, and for trusting me to be the one to open this dialogue with those who, like us, are searching for answers.

Dear Dad,

This book is for you.
I wish I had known then what I know now.
Maybe we could have talked more openly about your pain.
Maybe you wouldn't have felt so alone.

I hope you have found peace.

UNDERSTANDING SUICIDE

PROLOGUE

When I published the first edition of this book, in 2008, I had no idea how it would impact others. My initial intention was to give solace and information to those who, like me, had lost loved ones to suicide, not to share my individual story. But, when I handed its first version to my publisher, Luis Emediato, he immediately asked me why I hadn't mentioned my father's suicide. "The reader will never understand why you wrote this book if you don't." He was absolutely right. Every time someone contacts me about the book, the only chapters mentioned are the autobiographical ones.

Throughout the years, I have received hundreds of messages from individuals who are going through grief or are in such pain that they are contemplating suicide themselves. I feel honored to hear their heartbreaking accounts of broken relationships, parental neglect, financial difficulties, mental illness, and isolation. On one hand, the fact that they trust my ability to listen is quite touching; on the other hand, knowing that someone has reached such a state of despair they had to confide in someone they have never met always filled my heart with sadness because it just shows how alone they must feel.

In many instances, I have been contacted by readers who say that my book saved their lives. This usually happens with people who have decided to end their lives but are willing to give it a last chance. They browse the Internet, find my website, and buy the book. To think that my words can help reverse their sense of hopelessness is more than I ever hoped for this book. It was because of these exchanges that, in 2016, I decided to create a website in the hopes that by sharing what I know, I could reach a broader audience and touch more lives. Finally, in 2019, I worked on the English version of both the book - with new chapters and updated information - and the website. This is what you are holding in your hands.

Since the death of my father, in 2005, working on suicide prevention has become a personal cause, one that has filled my life with joy and accomplishments. It has also led me to change professions from being a journalist to becoming a therapist. This has been one of the best decisions I have made in my life, one that has transformed the way I relate to others. Since then, I have earned a degree in Psychoanalysis, in Brazil, and a Master's degree in counseling in the United States.

During the last few years, being able to share what I have learned has been a great privilege to me. My goal is to continue connecting with people, to hear their stories, and to hopefully help them find meaning in their lives.

My websites:
www.understandsuicide.com (English)
www.prevencaosuicidio.blog.br (Portuguese)

"Suicide is a word you whisper."

Dr. Brian Goff

UNDERSTANDING SUICIDE

Introduction

Mahnaz was six when her mother doused herself and her three children with gasoline. She wanted all of them dead. She was tired of her husband's infidelity and the physical aggression that came whenever she complained about it. Her actions would serve as punishment; that should show him that she was also capable of extreme measures. Mahnaz still cannot recall the events of that day, only that she wasn't afraid. At some point, she remembers feeling sorry for her mother. Her mother had been crying a lot, and then suddenly left, making her way to her own parents' home. The children were left in the house, alone and drenched in fuel.

Mahnaz always viewed her mother as the victim of a brutish, unfaithful, and authoritarian man. He abused the children as well, which passed for teaching respect. In Iran, this male behavior is tolerated, and women are taught to stay quiet and remain married. It did not take long for her mother to return home. For a few days, an aunt came to the house to take care of them. She was just as rigorous as their father and lacked any affection. Her father couldn't take it for too long, however, and begged his wife to return home. Little changed, though, and the years passed until Mahnaz turned twelve.

One day, when she got home from school, she noticed that something was amiss. Family members were coming and going, the phone was ringing off the hook, and her mother seemed extremely upset. The atmosphere was heavy, but she had no idea what was happening. This went on for a few weeks. No one ever said anything openly, but she could hear them whispering around the house.

Mahnaz only found out the reason for all the tension when she had a small row with her mother, who, in an outburst of anger, yelled, "You are just like your stupid father and his other wife and daughter." She was stunned and could not grasp at first what her mother was saying. When she finally did, she was furious. So that was it, her father had a double life, a second family. "We have to go there and kill them all, mother." She grabbed a knife, and they went in search of her father.

The strongest memory she has of the moments when they arrived at the other family's house was the pain she felt when a woman opened the door and she saw her father holding a baby. Until that day, she had been Daddy's little girl. But no more, and seeing that, her world collapsed. For a few minutes, they destroyed everything they could get their hands on. The woman ran to the neighbor's house, taking the baby with her. Mahnaz's parents had a terrible fight, and as they were leaving, she told her father, "I hope you die." Things immediately changed for the worse.

Her mother suggested she would take care of his baby as if she were hers, but under the condition that he left his lover and came back home. He did not accept this, and so Mahnaz's mother left. From that day on, the children were all alone in the house, this time without their father, who'd hired some help to take care of them. The few times he came to visit, he and the children fought, and he ended up spanking them.

A few months later, her father bought a new house, in a rich Teheran neighborhood, and all the children moved in with him, his new wife and their baby. Mahnaz and her brothers were not happy with the situation; they did not accept the "new" family, and ended up having to live in the basement of the new house.

Mahnaz became aggressive and rebellious. Her mother used to call every day and instruct her on how to behave. That included adding hair to her dad's wife's food, disobeying her stepmother at every opportunity, and not accepting any of her efforts at being nice. Her brothers spent their days outside, playing with their friends, which was something she couldn't do, as an Iranian girl. Her mother didn't care about her, and when she called, all she wanted was to hear about her dad's day-to-day life with his new wife. Mahnaz did not speak to her father. In less than a year, her life had turned upside down, and she felt lost and alone.

It didn't take long for all that to be reflected in her studies. She started missing classes and would wander around the city instead. Mahnaz didn't care about her father's aggressiveness anymore. The last drop came during a row with her stepmother, after which she decided to teach the whole family a lesson, so she went to the bathroom and swallowed every medication she could find, which amounted to around two hundred pills.

Mahnaz was talking to her mother on the phone when her mother noticed something was not right in her daughter's voice. She could not articulate her words right. There was no one else at home at this point, so her mother called Mahnaz's uncle and said. "If something happens to my daughter, I will kill all of you." When he reached the house, he found his niece on the floor, unconscious.

Two days later, she woke up in the hospital and realized her plan hadn't worked. All she wanted was to have her stepmother blamed for her suicide attempt. Maybe if that happened, her father would leave her and go back home, where normal life could resume, no matter how complicated that 'normal' had been.

Instead, her life had become even more miserable. Three months later, she decided she really did want to die. She knew where her father kept the opium, Iran's middle-class drug of choice, so without second thoughts, Mahnaz swallowed everything she found and immediately started feeling sick. She then went to the neighbor's house for help and was taken to the hospital.

In the hospital, her father told her, "I hope you die. Now all the neighbors know what you did. You ruined our family's reputation." Six months later, Mahnaz and her brothers were sent to India. For three years, she cried daily. She was away from all her friends and family, and she implored her father to bring her back to Iran, but her pleas went unheard. While she lived in India, she engaged in several self-destructive behaviors. She spent months self-mutilating, cutting her wrists and arms repeatedly. Everyone knew but no one talked about it, including her mother when she came to visit. Everyone insisted on acting as if nothing was happening.

After the self-mutilating phase, Mahnaz spent the better part of six months sleeping. She found a way to buy Valium in the black market and stockpiled it, gradually upping the dosage. Sometimes, she would wake up crying, then would take more Valium and fall asleep again. When she, at last, chose to stop, she had lost a lot of weight and had no energy.

At sixteen, Mahnaz decided she had to change her life, leave the past behind and recover. She tried applying for visas to several European countries and was granted one from England. She asked her father to let her go, and he acquiesced. Currently, she is a psychologist and lives in an upper-middle-class neighborhood in London.

One of her brothers moved in with her. She wanted to provide them with the opportunity she had. They had become addicted to drugs, and one of them had almost died from an overdose. In 2006, her father almost died, and Mahnaz was the one who nursed him back to health. She ultimately reconnected with the entire family, including her stepmother and sister.

When I interviewed her, she still had recurring episodes of depression, but continued to follow her treatment. The last time she was in crisis, her sister - who became a close friend - went to London to help take care of her. She is optimistic about the future and has no regrets. Mahnaz's family views her with pride for overcoming her problems and rebuilding her life.

Silent determination

Quite unlike Mahnaz, Jose Romero had a happy childhood. He grew up in the countryside of Pernambuco, a state in the Northeast of Brazil, in a town where the houses have backyards and no surrounding walls, and everyone goes from house to house as if the whole neighborhood were one big family.

I interviewed two of his sisters, Alexandrina (his twin) and Celia, and neither remember any moments of crisis or problems during the course of their childhood. They all played together in their shared backyards, climbing trees and playing ball. It was a healthy and free lifestyle.

Jose was a shy person, but nothing out of the ordinary; he was a good student and read compulsively. "He was brilliant," the sisters report, and they had no reason to worry. Until, that is, he reached adolescence. At that point, his shyness started affecting his life. Jose had few relationships and showed signs of irritability.

For a while, he got upset about their parents' dedication to religion, which he found to be a waste of their energy. He did not believe in God. The first signs of this were when, during a discussion, he yelled at his father, criticizing his faith and religious practices—something he had never done before. Jose slowly became more isolated. The family decided to take him to a psychologist in Recife, the state capital. He was eighteen at the time of the visit.

Soon after, the whole family moved to Recife. Thinking back, Celia believes that it was during adolescence that Jose started showing signs of depression, becoming progressively more introspective despite maintaining a certain balance in his external life. He still had friends— "Few, but loyal ones," says Alexandrina.

His first undergraduate studies were in Philosophy, but he never finished, instead changing his major to Languages. He had difficulties carrying out projects and was not a practical person. Jose never learned to drive and remained at his parents' home until he was forty-three. His apartment was like a library, with books everywhere, but he was unable to operate a stove.

His relationship with the family was close and affectionate, even though he was naturally quiet and reserved. When I talked to Celia, she remembered the many times he had called her, saying he wanted to speak with her, but when he got to her house, he would say very little. He was an extremely private man.

Throughout his adult life, Jose went to several doctors and tried some treatments, including medication. During one of these doctor visits, he got particularly upset with the psychiatrist's suggestion that not only was he depressed but that he also presented several symptoms of schizophrenia, a diagnosis he could not accept.

He was never able to follow any treatment properly. Jose was afraid of taking medication, partly because he could not bear the idea of becoming dependent on it. Despite his resistance, he continued actively looking for a treatment that would cure him.

In 2002, when he was forty-six, Jose called Celia, once more saying he had something he wanted to talk to her about. "He came here, said nothing, and left," she remembers. A few minutes later, Celia got another call from their father, saying that Jose had arrived at their home and was extremely nervous. He had gone into a bedroom and, when he came out, they could see he had cut his wrists.

They took Jose to the hospital, but soon he was back at home. From that day on, the family was more watchful and often worried about him. His psychiatrist suggested group therapy, which he went to only once. He did not say a word during the session, though privately, to his sisters, he kept complaining about the medication.

In the following year, there was another suicide attempt, this time with medication. Once more, he was taken to the hospital. Alexandrina remembers being very angry at him and saying, while he was still in the hospital, that the "third time is the charm." Unfortunately, she was right, but no one could have imagined how traumatic his method would be to the family.

In January 2005, Jose spent a month at his twin's home on the beach. During that month, they enjoyed the sea, read books, had long talks, and enjoyed movies and restaurants. Alexandrina was a little worried about his weight loss but didn't think there was anything serious happening. There were no signs of what was to come.

In the following month, Jose spent the carnival weekend with his girlfriend and seemed to be doing well. He wasn't, however. One day that February, Celia got several calls from him while running some errands. She called him back as soon as she got home. A few minutes later, he rang the bell at her home. They sat down to talk, but the conversation only lasted around five minutes. He talked about medication and was very irritable. Again, he insisted he wasn't going to take the pills anymore. He had stopped treatment a month earlier.

For the first time, Celia, who always tried to convince him that taking medication would be temporary, was firm and told him he was sick, and that he would need to take the pills for the rest of his life. For the last time, Jose told her he would not become dependent on drugs. He got up, walked to the balcony, and jumped out, falling twenty floors to his death.

Celia has few memories of what followed in the immediate aftermath once she noticed what was happening. She remembers trying to call her husband while running to try to save her brother. But there was not enough time; everything happened too quickly.

Knowledge matters

The distance separating the Iranian Mahnaz and the Brazilian Jose Romero is not a geographical one. On one side, we have a girl who grew up tormented by violence and lack of love. On the other, a boy who had difficulty dealing with people, with everyday pressures and most importantly, with his own emotions. Each dealt with their pain in the only way they were able to. Mahnaz externalized her feelings by being aggressive, rebellious, and self-destructive, while Jose withdrew from everyone, internalizing his suffering and insecurities.

At sixteen, the Iranian girl decided she needed to start over, moving to another country. She found it difficult to adapt and changed schools several times. At the same age, the Brazilian boy began to withdraw and show signs that his perceived shyness might be symptoms of something more serious. The family was sensitive to his cry for help and took him to Recife for psychological treatment. Mahnaz's family did the opposite, sending her away and practically abandoning her.

In these two cases, we have young people who, at some point in their lives, were diagnosed with depression. But Jose never accepted the diagnosis. He believed he would become dependent on the medication, so he fought against his mental illness. Mahnaz followed her treatment, then studied the subject during her psychology training, and today she works in the mental health field.

When I think about these two stories, one of the central factors that differentiates Mahnaz and Jose is the degree of resistance regarding the understanding of mental illnesses. I truly believe that when we are able to make sense of a painful moment in our lives, dealing with the challenges that come with it becomes more manageable; it also helps us make informed choices, no matter how hard they might be.

For Mahnaz, studying about depression set her on a healing path, while for Jose, his defiance kept him at a distance from the possibility of a more rewarding future. Maybe he would have followed the treatment if he had known that untreated depression is a major risk factor for suicide, or that antidepressants must be taken rigorously; otherwise, withdrawal can have serious consequences on the psyche. It is impossible to know now, but I truly believe that a lack of awareness regarding mental health is detrimental to the prevention of suicide. I often think about the impact it would have made in my own father's death had I known what I know now, had I been able to pass it along to him. Would he still be alive?

After my father's suicide, I embarked on a painful, albeit necessary quest to grasp what had happened to him. I had so many questions, but in Brazil, there were no answers, no books on the subject. So I bought several from the United States and England, countries where the field of suicidology is quite advanced. It was this void of knowledge in my country that inspired me to write this book; I knew that there were thousands of people like me who needed some degree of understanding, and with it, solace.

Like everything that is fearsome, talking about suicide is something most people avoid. But the weight of silence is devastating and prolongs the long chain of suffering surrounding this kind of loss; it undermines those who consider taking their own life; it prevents friends and family from providing comfort and support; and lastly, it increases the suffering of those who lose someone to suicide. To each of these individuals, I have dedicated at least one chapter of this book. It is my way of honoring them and all who had the courage to come forward and share their pain with me.

No one is free from experiencing this nightmare, but I am positive that access to information can radically change this scenario. And this is what I intend with this book: to promote a wide and dynamic debate so that cases like Jose Romero's may turn into models of transcendence, such as what happened to Mahnaz.

In the following pages, you will get in touch with an issue that regularly shakes the very foundation of our human existence. The French philosopher Albert Camus once stated that suicide is the only truly serious philosophical problem. In my experience working in the field, self-inflicted death is highly stigmatized; it is certainly a frightening subject, but we need to look it in the eye.

Silence creates the perfect environment for the proliferation of suicide; ignorance feeds it, and it is my hope that this book will help set a path to a more compassionate understanding of this heartbreaking topic.

CHAPTER ONE

My Story

On January 10, 2005, I woke up to a phone call from my sister, Renata. Crying uncontrollably, she told me that our father had killed himself with a self-inflicted gunshot to the head. At the time, I was on vacation in Miami, and despite my best efforts to get back home to Recife, I wasn't able to arrive in time for his funeral. That day, searching for answers, I began my journey into the painful and complex world of suicide. Not only was I looking for what leads someone to take their own life, but more importantly, I wanted to know if and how it could be prevented. What I discovered was that in order to understand my father's irreversible choice, I had to go deep into my memories of our time together, and this journey required me to face my own childhood memories and our family dynamics. Most importantly, I would need to dig into my father's ghosts.

My journey to the past began by looking into my relationship with my mother; we have always had a special and intimate connection, since birth. On July 25, 1967, after her water broke, she was taken to a simple maternity hospital in Afogados—a neighborhood of Recife, a city in the Northeast of Brazil—thinking that my birth would be quick like my older sister's. She worried that it all would happen too quickly, so she rushed to the nearest hospital without waiting for her brother-in-law, Adisio, to arrive. He was the family's official obstetrician, but was in the middle of a work shift in another hospital, so she went to the hospital alone.

Her concerns were unfounded; there was plenty of time for him to arrive. For hours, I simply refused to leave her womb. That night, my uncle spent over seven hours applying pressure to my mother's belly in a useless effort to help me crown. Every time he managed to place me in the right position, he would ask my mom to push, but I would turn and roll in protest back into her uterus.

Unfortunately for my mother, the worst was yet to come. Back in 1967, women used to stay at the hospital for eight days after the delivery. Thus, my mother had to remain in a less-than-ideal maternity ward that had only four private rooms, none of which had the luxury of a private bathroom. If only she had known in advance how troublesome my delivery would be, she would certainly have gone to another hospital. Our struggle ended up lasting the whole night. On the following day, my uncle gave up and opted for a caesarean section. At around 7.30 a.m., despite my brave protests, I was delivered into the world.

As a baby, I was very tiny, skinny and quiet—so little and light that, when we left the hospital, my father carried me on his forearm. At that time, we lived in Rosarinho, a suburb of Recife, in a house owned by my mother's dad. My parents had been married for only two years, and I had been one of those common "accidents," the result of the rhythm method, a faulty one at best.

Renata was an unsettling ten-month-old baby; she took up every minute of my mother's time. Meanwhile, I kept trying to figure out ways to get her attention. Since I was the quiet one, instead of making noise or crying, I got her attention by always getting sick. I couldn't hold anything in my stomach, breast milk included. In retrospect, I see clearly that my goal was to keep her physically and emotionally tuned into me, and this behavior continued through adolescence. Over time, I became an expert in manipulating her love.

From Rosarinho, we moved to another one of my grandfather's houses in Dois Irmãos—a neighborhood that at the time I thought was the closest you could get to heaven, because it was located on the top of a hill. For my mother, though, it was more like hell. The bus came by only a few times a day, and we lived far from everything and everyone we knew.

We'd moved there because my parents needed to save money in order to build our home, so there was no extra cash for renting a place. By then, I was almost five years old and continuing to switch illnesses in order to get my mom's attention. Due to my complicated medical history, my mother was quite well-known among the city's pediatricians. Her latest pursuit at the time was to find an asthma specialist.

I don't hold many memories from those days, but my mom never forgot those three insane years. She hated animals, spent the whole day by herself, had no car, and had only one neighbor close by. She recalls one day when my father arrived and found the whole family sitting on top of a table, my mother desperately trying to keep all of us there for hours. Under the table was a white-eared possum, looking calmly at us. For her, that was the last straw—we had to move out.

It turned out that the animal scare was only an excuse. Later in life, she confessed that by then, she feared for my health, and one of the doctors had prescribed the sea air to improve my breathing. Fortunately for my parents, our home was nearing completion in Boa Vi-agem—a neighborhood at the seashore, which today is a very expensive place to live. At that time, it was a remote, sparsely inhabited area where people spent their summer vacation. My father yielded to our mother's arguments and, once again, we packed our bags and left.

Truth be told, the house was actually a beautiful, unfinished project, hardly suitable for a family. It had no doors, not even a front door, and only the kitchen and one of the bathrooms were fully completed. The contractors had worked for five years, but on the weekends only, because we could not afford more than that. But that was what we had, so we took it. Against all odds, however, we kids were as happy as kids can be. It was a spacious place that offered all the attractions a child needs to have an unforgettable childhood: mud, tall trees, neighbors and freedom. And no white-eared possums.

The location of the house was a curious one. We lived right in the middle of three massive slums named *Entra Apulso, Mata Sete*, and *Planeta dos Macacos*, all direct references to danger, to drug dealing and crime.

Although drug dealers currently run these communities, things were different then. We could walk freely, going in and out of our neighbors' homes, chatting along the way. We also witnessed little violence, if any at all. The nearest paved street was miles away, and the muddy alleys were inhabited by stray dogs, chickens, and horses. Yes, horses. Believe it or not, the locals used them as a means of transportation.

One of my favorite memories of those years was playing a game with my sisters. The aim was to see who could reach a set destination with no mud on their feet—an impossible task, of course. The loser was the one with the dirtiest feet. Needless to say, no shoes were allowed; that would take away all the fun. This required a kind of dance, an exercise of balance accomplished by taking long steps and high jumps among the rocks, planks or garbage that lay around the streets. Sometimes, I would compete against myself, trying to step on the least number of obstacles possible until I arrived at my favorite stop: Edite and João's general store.

The place was an absolute paradise. Besides numerous cachaça bottles—the Brazilian national alcoholic beverage made of sugar cane—the store had all kinds of treasures hanging from the ceiling: popcorn, candy, chocolate, gum, cotton candy, lollipops, and my favorite of all, giant meringues, which gave a touch of color to the place. I can still taste the mixture of sugar and artificial coloring melting in my mouth.

Our favorite day was Friday, when my dad distributed our allowance. We would collect our coins and run over there to buy sweets. In truth, what we called the store was actually one of the rooms of their tiny wooden house that they had converted into the shop. Each one of us would buy so much candy that we needed to fold our T-shirts in order to hold them together on our way home.

Renata always found a way to raise some money during the week, and she would generously share amongst us. The extra cash was usually "found" in my father's pockets when he naively hung his pants on the bedroom door after arriving from work. Edite and João loved this habit of his, often profiting from it.

Friday had an extra-special touch for me, because it was the day of the week when my mother did her grocery shopping, and she usually allowed me to go to the supermarket with her and Aunt Nati, her closest friend. Those were hours of ultimate happiness. My sisters and brother hardly ever came with us, so it was a valuable time to spend with my mom without the need to share her with others. Once back home, we would store the groceries in the pantry and spend the afternoon chatting, eating, and having fun. Nothing could take me away from them—there was no better place to be.

Being by her side wasn't only pleasant; it also helped me avoid my father's presence. Taking part in her routine allowed me to relax and let go of the tension that consumed me when he arrived home and started drinking.

Being around my dad was never comfortable. The more he drank, the more I would distance myself from him. He never got aggressive or abusive in any way, quite the contrary—he got clingy and melodramatic. The unwanted *I love you's*, the hugs, the change in his behavior made me despise the man he was in those moments, and miss the father I had momentarily lost to alcohol. Those feelings were somewhat sublimated when I was by my mom's side. That was my safe place.

In our large yard, we had trees of all kinds and sizes. From a child's perspective, we lived in a forest. My parents dedicated many hours to taking good care of it, planting mango, coconut, guava, and many Brazilian native fruits. Among those trees, we came up with another family competition: who was the best climber? In that regard, Eveline put us all to shame. We could never beat her. To my mother's despair, she had been an avid climber since she was very little. Mom loved to tell us the story of her crawling on the refrigerator's shelves way before she could properly walk. My little sister always loved being in high places— maybe this partially explains her choosing to be a pilot later in life.

The centerpiece of our yard was a huge mango tree, my pride and joy. We used to climb up to the top of that tree, carrying with us salt and knives (I'm sure my mom wasn't aware of the blades). As peculiar as it may sound, unripe mangoes taste delicious when sprinkled with salt.

The mango tree was our crucial ally on another front: It was also there that we hid when we did something wrong. Since my mother would never dare to climb the tree, we could stay there risk-free. All we needed to do was give her some time to cool down, then come down as if nothing had happened.

Right across from our front gate lived Maria and Duval, a couple who were dear to us. Back then, there were no washers and driers, so she took care of our clothes; her husband was a painter who often helped my dad retouch the house and do some minor maintenance work. Another constant presence in our home was "Grandpa," who lived in the house across the street.

We called him that because he was a very old man with a scary hunchback who appeared to be 110 years old. He was some kind of handyman, performing jobs that ranged from gardening to taking care of us when our parents had a night out. He loved my parents and would find any excuse to be with us all day. When working as our sitter, he sat in the rocking chair on the front porch, where he mostly slept until they came back. Grandpa adored my mother. She made him feel at home.

A step away from Maria's house lived a hysterical, loud woman whose name I never knew. She lived with her daughter, Joelma. The whole neighborhood knew her daughter's name, because the crazy lady spent the day shouting it. Joelma was the most popular girl in our neighborhood. Well, not her specifically, but her name for sure. I don't remember ever seeing her—maybe her mother held her captive, or maybe Joelma was only a product of that neurotic woman's imagination.

One more local character deserves to be mentioned: Luis, an authoritative man who maintained order and safety in our neighborhood. Because of him, nobody dared to be out of line. He laid out the rules. For example, no home breaking, robbing, mugging, or doing drugs among the neighbors. His unwritten but strictly enforced laws were always followed; he kept crime from running loose and drowning our community. Luis respected my parents, and because of his presence, we could leave our doors wide open for many years, something unimaginable in Brazil, even then. But that was bound to change, even in our special neighborhood.

When the mall was built, the local residents had to live with a constant reminder of a world that they couldn't attain. The mall started to gentrify the area. Flashy cars, high-end homes, and sleek buildings started to pop up everywhere, and with them, the social disparity became painfully clear. After all, for many years, we were the only middle-class family our neighbors knew. With time, Luis's rules started to crumble, and I was the first victim of the impending change.

One day, when I was around thirteen years old, I was mugged by two armed men on the way home from school. They took my watch, which I had just received as a gift from my dad. Nothing fancy, it was made of plastic, but it had a sentimental value to me. When I arrived home, crying, I told my parents, and soon enough, the news had spread within the community.

Hours later, Luis came to our home, holding a teenager by the arm. He had a gun with him. My father summoned me; they wanted to know if this boy had been the one who took my watch. I recognized the robber, but I kept the information to myself and said no. Somehow, I knew that by saying yes, I would be putting that boy's life at risk. No one ever said that, but I just knew.

A few days later, again on my way home, the same boy sat by my side on the bus. We both recognized each other, and I could tell that he was uncomfortable with the situation. I started a conversation and, as an icebreaker, I asked him to walk me home. "I'm afraid to walk alone at this hour," I said. Without looking me in the eye, he agreed to accompany me. We walked in silence, and he left me at my doorstep. After that day, I never saw him again.

Back in our whimsical yard, another habit that kept me entertained was to sit on the top of the brick wall that surrounded our property. I would get there by climbing the guava tree that overlooked João and Edite's store. They were the only residents who had a record player; his was a modern model, with built-in speakers. "Fancy stuff," my father used to say. I would spend hours there, watching people come and go, kids leaving with candies and smiles on their faces, all to the sound of a few songs repeated countless times.

I would stay there eating guava and paying close attention to the neighbors. João would play songs he knew were favorites of the drunks who gathered at his general store, getting wasted, baffled by the sounds that came out of the record player. It was marketing at its best, from the most professional entrepreneur in the community.

My preference for being alone alternated between moments of peace and quiet, when I was playing with my dolls, and moments of anxiety, when the family balance was shaken, which was usually provoked by my father's drinking. In my early years, I was a frightful, insecure child, extremely sensitive to his moods and how they affected our lives. We were all impacted by this, and in many ways, our family reproduced the common roles played by families of alcoholics.

It didn't take much for me to get angry with my father. Sometimes, all he needed to do was talk to me. My rejection was so deep-rooted that the moment I heard his voice, I would mumble something, turn around, and cut the conversation short. Then, guilt would take over, because I loved my dad and I felt horrible for mistreating someone who tried so hard to win my heart. At times, feeling ashamed for my behavior, I would force myself to be affectionate with him, but that never lasted very long. When I would go too far and hurt my dad's feelings, my mother would call it to my attention and make me participate more actively in the family's routines.

There was a lot of love among my siblings and me. Renata had a tomboy attitude—no time for sweet talk or the usual behavior expected from girls. We still laugh about one anecdote from when she was a young child. One of our aunts insisted that Renata give her a kiss, something she rarely did. When Renata realized that there was no way out, she approached her slowly, and instead of kissing my aunt, she mischievously licked her cheek, laughing her heart out at her trickery.

Although she did not usually play the typical role of older sister, Renata was extremely protective of me. As often happens with siblings, we used to fight a lot. Since Renata and I were practically the same age—a narrow ten-month difference—we used to play together, and we shared the same group of friends. Eveline, on the other hand, was four years younger than me and, for obvious reasons, we did not want her around.

Sometimes, we would lock ourselves inside a room and play with friends, while Eveline would knock on the door asking in vain to get in. This happened with some regularity, which led her to come up with what she thought was the perfect revenge. In her mind, our friends were the reason why we rejected her, so she decided that by keeping them away, she would regain our attention. All she needed to do was to stop them from coming into the house.

Eveline's method was fast, effective, and quite painful. When she knew that someone was coming over, she would position herself by our front gate and wait until the kids crossed it, and then she would throw big rocks at them. Her revenge worked for a while, but once the victims became aware of her strategy, they would scream for us from the street, and we could tell our mother, who would come and fetch my sister before she could hurt them.

In my family, everybody had a nickname, some cute, some not so much. Eveline had three: Porrote, Capota-choca, and Little Princess. The first one because of her flat nose at birth; the second, a reference of her short temper, and the last one because she has always been beautiful. Her golden, long curly hair and blue eyes made her look like an authentic fairytale princess.

Everybody called me Paula, with the exception of Renata, who came up with the nickname Nina, which prevailed until well into our adulthood. My dad called me "Old Lady with a Bun"; old lady because I was born with an old spirit, and bun because it was how I always tied my hair. I still do. Adisio, the youngest and the only boy, went by Dido, and Renata was known as Tata. Dad had an extra nickname for her: "Gurunga," which doesn't mean anything really, he totally made it up. We never knew the reason for that name, but it sounded funny and sweet.

Eveline could be quite strange sometimes. When my Uncle Carlos came to visit us from Campinas—a city in São Paulo, in the Southeast—which happened once a year, she would run to the side of the house and bury her face in the sand. With Uncle Carlos came his daughter Eveline, our all-time favorite cousin. My parents liked to honor their relatives, so my sister was named after her. Eve, which is what we still call her, made all our dreams come true. She was also a great photographer, and to this day, the best pictures we have of our childhood were taken by her. Having Eve around left us ecstatic, because she loved sewing princess dresses and ballet costumes. She was always a very talented designer and eventually ended up becoming a costume designer.

I'll never forget one of the tutu skirts she created for me. It was made out of pink puffed tulle, with small metal bells around the waist that tinkled while I spun around the house, listening to classical music and dancing ballet. Being a ballerina was my childhood dream, and Eve, very aware of each of our wishes, turned our world into pure fantasy and magic. With her help and love, we all accomplished our dreams to the fullest. Hers was simple: to see her little cousins happy.

Being the youngest and the only boy, Dido was left alone most of the time. His closest pal was my father, who was always ready to indulge my brother's whims. Making kites was his specialty. He had a very good eye for creative shapes and colors, and he assembled beautiful kites that flew like birds. He also bought wooden cars and planes so they could piece them together. Dido was very welcome, since my father had always longed for a son.

As a child, my brother was a handful. He wouldn't stand still and seemed to fear nothing. No fear, no limits. Wanting something was the same as having it, in his mind; all he needed was a careful plan—exchanging my mother's pans and kitchen gadgets for cotton candy, for example. In a way, apart from the anger at his lack of concern for others, I envied his view of life, because it was quite uncomplicated and straightforward. The word "no" didn't exist in his dictionary. It just didn't play a part in Dido's life.

He had an impressive power of persuasion. It wasn't as if he had indisputable arguments, not at all, but he was so insistent that he just wore people down. He would ask for something repeatedly for hours, until we budged and acquiesced . On the other hand, he was by far the most loving and charming among us. Dido had a kind and gentle heart and was never angry for long. Everybody loved him.

By the side of our home, my dad built a large swing for us. It was one of the few places where we all played together. One of us would usually push my brother while the others swung by themselves. Over time, we got bored and decided to turn the swing into a gymnastics bar. It seemed simple to us: just unhook the chains that held the swings, and we had a perfect metal bar. We would climb on the swing top, which was around nine feet tall, to impersonate Nadia Comaneci, the Romanian gymnast who was the first to be awarded a perfect 10 at the Olympic Games. I remember trying to keep balance on the bar—more like tightrope walking than gymnastics, for sure. Miraculously, there were never any accidents, though I'm pretty sure we never told our parents about the adventure.

Right across from the swing there was a concrete mixer, a big yellow device with a revolving drum used to mix cement. It was a leftover from the endless construction of our home. The machine's owner asked us to keep it for a while but never came back for it, so it became one of our favorite toys. The three of us would climb inside the drum while the fourth rotated it as fast as possible. The point was to pretend we were on the most dangerous ride of an amusement park. It was also used for small pranks, such as leaving one of the siblings in there, which was quite easy, because unless the rest of us lowered the drum, there was no way to get out.

In our private amusement park, there was also a concrete shelter used to protect the water pump. By stepping on it, we were able to climb the wall that surrounded our home. Once we were there, we would pretend to be tightrope walkers—with no balancing poles, of course. When that got boring, we started to try flying.

At that time, we were crazy about the *Flying Nun* sitcom, the one with Sally Fields portraying a nun who could fly by moving her head and holding her cornette. We made several hats that looked like hers and performed the same moves, with high hopes that the wind would help us take off. Needless to say, the attempts were futile, but the funny thing for me to remember is that we would compete on the height each of us accomplished. We all swore we had flown a little bit more than the others.

When it comes to school, I have very few memories; the most vivid of them is probably the long, pointy red toenails of my Portuguese teacher, Muriel. I got so fixated on her nails that I could barely focus on her lessons—I've always sat in the front row, and still do. Those nails scared the hell out of me, which contrasted with the way I felt about Muriel as a person. She was a sweet, loving and playful teacher.

In Brazil, kids don't stay in school from 8 a.m. to 3 p.m. as they do in the United States. We have to choose between morning, from 7.30 a.m. to 12 p.m., and afternoon, from 1 p.m. to 5.30 p.m., so lunch is never served there. We did have a snack break, though—our parents gave us money for it, but it was never enough to get all the treats we wanted. Again, Renata's generosity would come to the rescue. She always had some extra money to share with us—and our father always had a little less in his pockets as a result. I've always wondered if he was aware of her night visits. I can't imagine him not knowing. Maybe he even left some spare change on purpose to make it easier for her to share with us. Dad always turned a blind eye to our mischiefs, and I certainly never had the guts to ask.

My mother was the center of my life; nothing distressed me more than seeing her upset. Pleasing her was my mission. She taught me how to cook at a young age, and by around thirteen, I could already cook lunch for the whole family by myself. The main reason I did that was to be around my mom. Her presence was soothing to me. Looking back, I see my mother as a wise woman, someone who could identify my needs and who knew how to deal with them in a very gentle way.

I don't want to give the impression that my father was absent in our lives; it was much the opposite. He always came home early straight from work and rarely went out by himself or to meet friends, and all of his entertainment included us. He was a very dedicated father and husband, focusing on pleasing all his children according to our individual tastes. With Renata, he would talk about music—Rock and Roll was her favorite—and books; with Eveline, it was quality snuggle time and storytelling; with Dido, endless sports and pranks. As for me, as much as he tried, we didn't spend a lot of time together, because I would simply not allow him in. I kept a distance.

Knowing what I know now, I see some of my attitudes as basic coping mechanisms. By avoiding my father, I avoided pain, something all of us do to some degree. There were other things I used to do that are borderline crazy, though. I will walk you through some of them, but let's start with the most reasonable ones first.

As a young girl, I was quite religious, something I learned by watching my pious grandmother, who went to church practically every day. Theoretically, my parents believed in God, but if I'm honest, I don't recall them ever talking about Him, so I created my own rituals. I prayed every night before going to bed. My ongoing chat with God was not a smooth one, though. There was a lot of tension in our nightly conversation, and I had quite a few unattainable requests to make.

Stirring in the background of my holy talks lay the two things I dreaded the most: the possibility of my parents' divorce, and that of my mother's death. Every night, on my knee— the ritual had to be performed kneeling down, otherwise it would not constitute a sacrifice, some-thing I associated with religion—I asked that neither of those things ever happened, particularly the latter. Nowadays, I can clearly see the strong contradiction of my relationship with my father and the fear of their divorce. On the one side, I rejected my dad, but on the other, when asking God to keep them together, I also wished to have him close by.

At some point in my childhood, I decided that the prayers and kneeling down were not enough to keep my mother alive anymore, so I came up with another repetitive ritual. I would write the letter M—the initial for mother, "mãe" in Portuguese—everywhere I went. It could be done on any surface: doors, windows, walls. This innocent habit was no nuisance to those around me, but I took it to extremes, which one time led my mother into a heated argument with one of my aunts. Looking back, she had all the reasons in the world to be angry with me.

It all happened on a Sunday, when we were visiting my mother's brother, Geraldo. Since one of the demands of my compulsion was that the M must be written sooner than later, I remember walking around the house, trying to find the perfect spot for the ritual to be performed. Suddenly, I saw a beautifully carved wooden chess board that my uncle had brought back from a trip to Asia. Each piece was a work of art, but all I could see was the board and its dozens of squares. "Perfect! I can write so many M's there", I thought. Undoubtedly, that would guarantee my mother years of perfect health, so I pushed all the pieces off the board, and with the metal bracelet I had on, I started carving each and every one of the squares with the letter M. When my aunt saw her beautiful chess board ruined, she came right after me, and my mom intervened in my favor. We ended up leaving their home, and they didn't talk to each other for months.

Sometimes, my mother would read bedtime stories to me. During those magical moments, I grasped her clothes, so that when she got up I would feel the motion and open my eyes. Then, I would say, anxiously, "I'm awake, Mom," and she would remain there for a while longer.

My perfectionist organization was way off the charts for a child. My wardrobe was impeccable, with clothes lined up orderly according to categories: tops, pants, skirts. Newly purchased items would stay wrapped in plastic. My mom was proud of that and made sure to reward me. Sometimes, when she went out to buy us new clothes—usually at Christmas and on our birthdays—she would bring me an extra piece. If my sister found out and protested, she would say that the reason why she got me additional items was because I was easy to please and never complained about her choices. Those were the pieces I carefully packed in plastic bags; it was my way to repay her care.

As a kid, I liked to draw, and I believe I had some talent. I did many "my family" drawings in school, but mine were different and odd, because they didn't include my siblings, the typical home with trees on the sides, or my father. There were only two of us, my mother and I, holding hands and wearing beautiful, princess-like dresses. These drawings were widely reproduced in letters I used to write to her. I wonder how none of the teachers ever questioned that.

Nowadays, these incomplete family drawings have become a joke between my siblings and I, so much so that on the Christmas of 2007, I made a card and sent it to my mom in Brazil, entitled "my family," with the whole crew. Under the drawing, I wrote, with a smiley face: "Some things never change. Others fortunately do."

The most popular doll at that time was Suzi, our tropical version of Barbie. The difference between them was the body shape, and it was not subtle at all—she was a clear representation of our culture. In comparison to the skinny body of the American doll, Suzi had wider hips, a proportionate head, and thicker thighs. Eventually, Barbie did take over the market, but by then, I was a young adult.

Later, in our teenage years, my sisters started thinking I was a hopeless psycho, but early on, as kids, they ignored my weirdness—maybe they didn't even notice it. Undoubtedly, my inner world was quite distressed, full of excessive fears and fantasies that were nothing more than escapes from the perception I had of my reality. I had an acute Cinderella complex—without a prince, because I didn't even think about it at the time. What I really wanted was the castle, the dresses, the horses, the sublime. In other words, I searched for a perfect world that can only be found in fairytales.

When things got too unsettling for me, I would put my headphones on—the large, old-fashioned ones—and listen to classical music. With Tchaikovsky on full blast, I would dance ballet around the world, walk through colorful parks and visit magic scenarios from books and movies. As usually happens with troubled kids, I also created an imaginary friend, and she followed me until my teenage years. Her name was Celia, and her persona was created based on my favorite TV show: *I Dream of Jeannie*. She had the same infinite powers as the character, and could do anything with the blink of an eye. When things got tough, Celia would remove me from the situation to a place where I would feel safe. I don't know much about imaginary friends, but I find it odd that mine was not physically present. We always spoke inside my head, so I must have known that she wasn't real. We lived together in a dark space in my brain, a parallel universe where suffering didn't exist. Just like Captain Tony Nelson in the TV series, I also punished Celia when she wasn't able to follow my requests. Whenever I got frustrated with her, I would send her back to her bottle. Poor Celia.

You may be thinking: what kind of pain does a little girl have if her childhood is surrounded by guava trees, a beautiful garden, swings, dolls, and a caring mother? This is where my father's story and mine intertwine. Hopefully, what led him to suicide will become clear in the next chapters of this book.

Teenage Years

Talking about my father is really hard. On the one hand, I fear that I may send an unfair message that would describe him as someone who only caused me harm. Nothing is farther from the truth. On the other, I can't overlook how much his alcoholism affected my psychological and emotional health, and the difficulty I had making peace with his addiction.

Childhood was probably the worst period, because those are the years that we search for references to mirror. Also, it is during these formative years that kids develop their attachment styles, and mine was definitely not a secure one. For children, caregivers are natural models; the way we relate to our parents can shape our future relationships. The manner in which I perceived my father was full of conflicts, a combination of love and rejection. In my eyes, he was everything I didn't want to become.

His alcoholism brought tension into the whole family. Our collective mood split between before and after my dad passed the acceptable threshold of alcohol consumption. Each one of us reacted in our own way. I believe mine was the most radical, ranging from aggression to coldness. When I couldn't hide in my room or climb the mango tree, I would treat him harshly—that is, if I talked to him at all. Most of the time, I ignored his presence in an attempt to push him out of my world.

Being alone in my room was one of the escapes I created to avoid the man on the other side of the door. The truth is, I knew very little about him, which only changed during the process of writing this book. In our home, practically nothing was discussed about his past, and most of what we heard from him ended up being a lie, as I found out during the interviews I conducted while working on this. Today, the way I would describe as follows: My father was a man who could never make amends with his past, someone whose family was distant from each other, and who was also a son of an alcoholic. His dad, I would discover later, lost everything he had to gambling. This had a profound effect on my father.

My dad was born in Reriutaba, a tiny town in Ceará—a state in Northeastern Brazil, 109 miles away from Fortaleza, the state capital. His parents were Gláucia and Homero. He was the oldest of four kids: two boys and two girls. My grandfather was a merchant, one of those people who are born to be a successful businessman. He owned several shops, selling shoes, fabric and other products. During his entrepreneurial years, he made a fortune, then lost it all to addiction.

Most of what I learned about my grandfather came from an interview I did with my Uncle Sobrinho, who was my fahter's best friend and who was married to Walquíria, my dad's closest sister. During our conversation, some of my uncle's revelations left me dumbfounded, particularly what he told me about my grandfather. All I knew about him before that moment had come from my dad.

My dad's story of him was quite limited: grandpa was filthy rich, lost everything to gambling, and died when my dad was twelve years old, which forced my dad to quit school and start working. So, I started the interview by asking him, "Tell me more about grandpa. I know nothing about him, only that he died when dad was twelve years old."

My uncle looked at me, surprised, and said, "Who on earth told you that? You were already born when your grandfather died, Paula. Your father was in his early thirties when that happened".

I'm sure you can imagine my disbelief at his words. After a few moments of silence, I called both my sisters and asked them what they knew. What I heard was a perfect repetition of my story, which was a relief, because by then I was questioning my own recollection. Maybe I had made all of that up, right? Wrong. When they confirmed my version, I immediately called my mother and told her about what had just happened. I asked her, "How come this very relevant issue never came up at home?" She was quite surprised herself that I had grown up with such a twisted interpretation of events, but very calmly stated that in our daily routine, my dad never brought up his family. For some reason, he seemed to be ashamed of them, so she decided to avoid it altogether. Talk about family secrets, huh?

In the course of our lives, we barely had any contact with Dad's family, apart from the few visits I made to Fortaleza, where I met his siblings Fernando, Laélio, and Carmelinda, my grandmother and cousins. Dad never said anything negative about them; I guess he was discreet about his grievances, a trait my Uncle Sobrinho knew quite well. Sobrinho and my dad met in the early fifties when they were both enlisted in the Army. He remembers the first time he saw my dad—it was on the day the troops were presented to their superiors. According to him, my dad stood out among thousand-plus young men because he was the only one dressed in an impeccable white suit, the same one he wore every day of that week.

Soon, everyone was curious about the man in white. Those dreaming of a military career wondered who that elegant man was, my uncle included. They ended up sharing a room when both of them were transferred to Crateús—a little town in Ceará—along with twenty other soldiers. Sobrinho remembers my father as high-spirited and extroverted, but never speaking about his family. "We slept side by side and were always together," he recalled. One day, my father asked my uncle to accompany him to the train station. That was where my uncle met my grandfather for the first time. Little did he know that years later, he would become his father-in-law.

Disciplined and smart, my father quickly acquired visibility in the military. He dedicated himself to study telecommunications, an area of great importance at the time. For him, it was a rare opportunity to learn, since his schooling had lacked technical skills. Although his father was very much alive after I was born, it seems that at least part of his story was true. He did have to work when he was twelve, but the reason was my grandfather's financial problems, not his death. That was the only period of his life he ever talked about, and always with sadness and sorrow.

His job was many miles away from his home, in a high part of the city. He walked to work, and his lunch was usually bread and bananas. That's what his life was reduced to, or at least that was all he ever told us, a clear demonstration of how traumatic it was for him. With my mother, it wasn't much different. She told me that even after their engagement, and five years of dating, she couldn't convince him to introduce her to his family. My grandpa passed away in 1972 when they already had three kids. My mom and the three of us never met him.

My parents met in Fernando de Noronha, an island in the Northeast of Brazil, which at that time was a military base. She was there to visit her sister, Yolanda, who lived on the island with her husband, Giovanni. There, at her sister's house, they first saw each other. After five years of going back and forth from Fernando de Noronha to Recife, my parents decided to get married. At first, her father Amaro didn't approve of their union. "He said that people only choose the Army when they aren't fit for anything else," recalls my mom. But soon, he grew fond of my dad. Over the years, my father earned everybody's love and respect.

From the beginning, my mother made it clear that if they ever got married, Dad would need to leave the Army, because she didn't want that lifestyle. My mom was very close to her family and loved Recife, so moving was out of the question. He abandoned his career and headed to Recife. I believe that leaving the military was a great loss for my father. He loved being in the military, and always talked about those years in the service with much pride—it was his true vocation.

One of the strongest images I have of him is him standing up any time the National Anthem was played, no matter where. He would immediately rise, place his hand on his chest, and sing. I witnessed this scene many times. My father wanted to be a military man, but his love for my mother was greater, and he decided to close that chapter of his life, but never managed to entirely. His efforts to keep it alive were often exaggerated. One of them became a family joke. After years humming the reveille early in the morning—a call used to wake military personnel at sunrise—my mother was finally able to convince him that there were more pleasant ways to wake us up.

My father was excessively organized. I used to wonder whether he had become that way because of the Army or the other way around—that is, perhaps he had been so successful in the military due to his discipline. I would guess the latter, because I cannot picture him being any different— everything he did was meticulously planned and executed. Timetables were carefully set up, even for the most trivial things. His office, a place where he would isolate himself, had hundreds of books, pictures and vinyl records. It was his sacred space, a large room built onto the back of our house. In the middle of it, there was a wide wooden desk with a world globe and a bust of Beethoven, his favorite composer.

It was there that my father spent most of the weekends reading, tending the family's accountability, and drinking. Always drinking. Inside one of the bookshelves, there was a compartment that was always locked, because it contained two large collections of medals and guns. On Sundays, barbecue day, he used to clean his revolvers, a habit he maintained for many years. When he was doing that, we knew we were to keep a distance.

In his office, my father studied a lot; he was a self-taught man. Education was central to him. His view was mirrored on my mother's side, where being educated was part of her immediate family's identity. We owe this legacy to my grandfather, Amaro. He inspired us all. Coming from a family of little resources, he held all kinds of manual jobs, such as shoe cleaner, wall painter, and salesperson. He could not go to school, but his priority was to make sure all ten of his kids would, including the women, which at the time was quite unusual. Getting a degree was a personal dream he managed to fulfill late in life.

At the age of seventy, and by then very successful, he graduated from law school. Six months prior, he had a stroke, which destroyed his ability to read, so for the last six months of the program, his schoolmates helped him finish the final tests. Making sure his kids graduated from college became a mission. Of the nine who reached adult life, six earned at least one university degree, including my mother.

Education was a main theme in my home as well, and when I refer to education, I mean it as a source of purpose, which is how both my dad and maternal grandfather saw it. My father spoke English fluently and was jokingly called "a walking encyclopedia" by his friends. My mom says that one of the reasons he took her family as his own was because he admired them intellectually, and looked up to her father's values.

One of the strongest memories I have of my dad was of him buried in his books. As I mentioned before, that room was his fortress. Sometimes, to my annoyance, he would want me to hear his detailed musical-history explanations of concertos and symphonies. Having been in the Army for fourteen years, he knew what every sound of Tchaikovsky's 1812 overture represented, depicting Russia's victory over Napoleon in the Battle of Borodino. "Hear the cannon shots in the background? It's the French troops advancing!" he would say, enthusiastically.

As much as I was fascinated by his office, the room was equally a source of discomfort, because it was there that I saw the worst versions of my father. I enjoyed hanging out with him, but only until I sensed his drinking was getting out of control. When that happened, I would do anything in my power to avoid that place.

I remember that many times, I wanted to be with my mother in her sewing room, which was next door to his office, but I knew that as soon as he saw me, he would invite me in, so I would make my way around the house to avoid him altogether. Sometimes, I took my chances tiptoeing so he couldn't hear me, but the path to the sewing room was covered in small, noisy gravel, so that was always a hard mission to accomplish.

I've spent a long time trying to convince myself that his addiction wasn't that bad and that his behavior could have been worse—after all, stories of alcoholic parents tend to involve violence and abuse, and that wasn't the case at all. But even though a child may not be able to verbalize it, the combination of love and alcohol doesn't feel genuine. When these two ingredients mix, the result is often a feeling of emptiness and repulsion.

After learning about his life, it became clear to me that his story was like many others. Addiction runs in families. He despised his dad's alcohol dependence but developed it himself nonetheless. The reason why he never allowed us to meet our grandfather was because he was a shameful mirror pointing to what my dad hated equally in himself. But he did what many addicts do—he carried on the generational legacy, inflicting the same trauma on us.

My escape strategy changed with time. When I was a kid, I transferred all my needs and expectations to my mother, which led to many affective distortions. I remember crying with those headphones on, constantly terrified by the idea that she could die and leave me with no escape route.

The make-believe world I lived in was also a way to get away from my perceived reality. Ballet classes were the perfect stage for my princess dreams; the sitcom *The Flying Nun* allowed me to venture away from anxiety and pain; classical music deafened me to the sounds I didn't want to hear. I remember one argument in particular. My parents were fighting in the kitchen—something they rarely did when we were around—and my dad, drunk, would throw lemons at a painting. That produced a loud bang that startled me, making my heart race. In my room, I would cover my ears in vein. Years later, my therapist associated that to the firework phobia I still have. It's a possibility.

My father's agony became quite visible when he got drunk. We never understood where this came from, since he never opened up to us, but it seemed like a deep-rooted attempt to fight painful memories, shadows from a past we never knew. When he got exhausted, he slept with his head over the desk, or just lay down anywhere in the house, on the floor, where he would stay until the following day. His unpredictability made me avoid bringing friends over, unless they were close enough not to care. Even so, I always preferred to go to their homes.

For years, I would leave the house on Friday and return on Sunday night. That was my way of bypassing the worst part of his addiction, the weekends, when he would drink non-stop. My Uncle Zeco and Aunt Lúcia's home was the number-one choice because of my dearest cousin, Deco, their middle son. He was one-of-a-kind: a little older than me, but with the wits of a premature adult. His demeanor was irresistible, always quite the charmer, and because of that, he collected girlfriends, which he loved to brag about. Deco was always in my home—he saw my father as his own and taught us a lot about life.

His sister, Cristina, was almost thirty at that time, an elder in my eyes. I admired her. She was a bookworm and very tidy. One of my greatest delights was to be with her in her room, a rare occurrence, because she was always immersed in books. I particularly remember her jewelry boxes, which were filled with delicate rings, earrings, and bracelets. I can still picture in detail a rhinestone necklace she had, and how I dreamed of wearing it with my imaginary ball dresses.

I never asked my mom whether or not she associated my weekend escapes with the difficulty I had being around with my father. I do know he missed me, because he used to complain about it to my mom. Once, I heard him say, "Why is Paula like that? She's always in her room, inside her own world with those bloody headphones on."

When he wanted to annoy me, he called me "invocada", which has no parallel in English. The word is a mixture of a person who holds a serious facial expression and has very little sense of humor. I hated that word. He did it with a touch of tenderness in his voice, though. I think it was just one of his ways to get my attention, something I rarely gave him. When he managed to irritate me, he would smile victoriously; after all, in those moments, I did pay attention to him. I was angry but undoubtedly connected to him.

When he was sober, we were able to enjoy our time together and build beautiful memories. Dancing was one of them. Neither my sisters nor my mother enjoyed dancing, so he used to teach me bolero and tango, his favorite genres. He truly believed he was good at it, but unless my memory fails me, he wasn't a very good dancer at all. But that didn't matter—for all I knew at the time, he was my Fred Astaire.

Music also worked as a hint to where his level of alcoholism was, and we were finely attuned to that. His musical taste would deteriorate according to how drunk he got. The day would begin with Beethoven, Tchaikovsky, Mozart, and Bach, and would end with Freddy Fender, a cheesy Mexican singer who mixed rock 'n roll with country music, if that's even possible.

Between the classical musicians and Mr. Fender, he listened to the legendary tango singer Carlos Gardel, his favorite for my lessons. By the side of his office desk, we would twirl around imaginary ballrooms, dancing to boleros, waltzes, and tangos, which he sang and translated to me. One of them was Gardel's *Por una cabeza* ("By a Head"), immortalized by Al Pacino in *Scent of a Woman*. I recall my disappointment when my father translated the lyrics to me—it totally ruined the romantic idea I had of it.

> *"Por una cabeza*
> *Todas las loucuras*
> *Su boca que besa*
> *Borra la tristeza,*
> *Calma la amargura"*

In free translation, it goes something like this: "By a head, I would do crazy things. Her kissing mouth erases the sadness, calms down the bitterness." I had always believed it was a song about the woman he loved, but my dad explained it was nothing but the despair of a horse gambler after losing "by a head." I didn't know it then, but this is one of the ways victory is measured in horse races. You can win by a head, a half-head, a neck, and so on. I was devastated and never danced to that song with the same passion after that.

His love for music was one of my father's greatest influences on all of us. He used to pay close attention to classical pieces, trying to identify the instruments and background effects. I listened to him with fascination— his knowledge of music truly amazed me. "Hear the violin? Now the oboe," he would say. He would alter the volume according to the piece's movement. As the tempo changed, from adagio to vivace, he would turn the sound up, reaching deafening heights sometimes. And I would stay there, eyes glued to him. Listening to music with my dad was a lively and unforgettable experience.

His love for knowledge and books took a while to catch up to me. Overall, I was an average student at best—I even flunked the seventh grade. At the time, in Brazil, if you got an F in any class, you had to repeat the whole year, though that has changed now. The funny thing is that the class I failed to pass was Portuguese. I was a bad writer, to say the least. After that experience, I became obsessed with the language, and years later, as if to prove that I could really do it, I became a journalist and writer.

Renata had a long history of bad grades, so repeating a school year wasn't exactly new to her. She tells me that when we got the school results and I found out that I didn't go through, I panicked. On the way home, I came up with apocalyptical fantasies: "I'm going to die!" I said, crying. Renata tried to bring me back to reality. "Calm down, this flunking thing is not the end of the world, let it go." But I was grieving. "God, I'm so stupid!" I screamed, desperate, all the way home.

From that day on, I became a top student (a little compulsive, I'll give you that), and I made it up through the following years, especially in Portuguese. I studied all the time, to the point that once, my mother threatened to pull me from Santa Maria, the most expensive, religious, and strict private school in Recife. I had won a scholarship there and had to study very hard to achieve the grades I needed in order to pass.

In my SAT year, I began to experience memory loss, a result of the mental exhaustion I had been putting myself through. I had created a study group with two other friends, Viberto and Saulo, brainiacs in math, physics, and Portuguese. We always studied together, and they were a great help in my adaptation to a school that was distant from my reality. The only subject I was better at than they were was English.

Most of the students at Santa Maria were wealthy; I remember the long lines of cars with private drivers dropping them off every morning. During the two years I was there, my last two of high school, I never mingled—I was shy and insecure. At recess, I preferred to stay in the classroom reading or just waiting for it to be over.

It was an uncomfortable environment, very different from the life I had outside of school. As much as I wanted to, I wasn't able to make new friends there. The year I enrolled, I already knew three students there, previous friends I had met through my sister Eveline. When I finished, those three were still the only ones I knew. Twenty years later, someone organized a reunion, and I was invited. It was like receiving an email by mistake—I had no idea who those people were, and never went to the party.

My language skills improved so quickly that I received a commendation for an essay contest in school. I could barely believe it when I saw it on the school's announcement board. To make things even better, the teacher read the piece aloud in the classroom so everyone could hear it. I felt shy receiving all that attention, but also extremely proud. Finally, my nightmare of the seventh grade had been left behind.

When it came to education, my father was very supportive—he would make any sacrifice to buy books and pay for extracurricular activities, which came around quite often. At times, we went through difficult financial hurdles, like when he had to be hospitalized to undergo a colostomy. It happened when he was in Fortaleza visiting his family. At that time, his best friend and business partner, Giovani, ran a successful furniture factory with him. When Dad fell ill and couldn't go to work, Giovani dissolved their partnership. That was one of the biggest disappointments in my father's life. They never talked again.

My father was unemployed for a couple of years after that, and until this day I don't know how we got by. It was a huge loss for all of us, because his friend was married to my mother's sister, Yolanda. Uncle Gionni and Aunt Lola (as we used to call them) owned a home where we used to go almost every weekend. It was a child's paradise: white, with towers, on the top of a hill overlooking a wooded area on the outskirts of Recife.

We also shared the same beach house on our vacation, as well as the same golf club. The breakup was radical. Once again, my father kept his pain to himself—he never told us what had happened. He just stopped talking about his lifelong friend and partner, without a word said. Giovanni's name was erased from our lives, and with that, our close relationship with Aunt Lola and our two cousins in that family, Renato and Ana.

Fortunately, at that time, I had been awarded two scholarships, one at Santa Maria, and another at Cultura Inglesa, a private English school, so those expenses were written off the bills. My mother helped the best she could, by sewing clothes for sale and by keeping a tight grip on our budget.

To my father, however, those years were extremely painful. He felt ashamed he could not provide us with the financial security we'd had in the past. He was an old-fashioned family man, always setting an example to others. Once again, his childhood trauma had come back to haunt him. In his distorted view, he had become his father, and nothing could be worse than that.

Sometimes, his pride went too far. With all the difficulties we were going through at that time, he refused to ask for help, and his attitude never changed. Uncle Sobrinho told me that in the last years of my dad's life, he knew that my father wasn't well and wanted to help him, but he was never able to do it, because my father wouldn't open up to him. I wish he had.

I have few recollections of him admitting to failure, and the ones I recall took place only in the last months of his life. By then, he had become so fragile that a sense of hopelessness had taken over—he saw no way out. During his unemployed years, he tried to hide from us what was happening, and he must have done a pretty good job, because I hold very few memories from that time. One stands out: my fifteenth birthday, which in Brazil is the equivalent of the American sweet sixteen or the Mexican Quinceañera. We celebrate it in high style, with luxurious dresses, gifts for the guests, music, and a night of dance—pretty much like a wedding.

My dream was to have one of those parties with fifteen girls at each side, all in white, a ribbon on the cake, a large ballroom, an orchestra, and dancing. At midnight, I would show up in my puffed dress and would dance with my father to one of his favorite waltzes. But the family budget couldn't afford the extravagance, so what I ended up having was a simple party in our home.

At midnight, I wore a dress borrowed from my cousin, and you know what? It was amazing all the same. We danced all night long. Sady, Renata's boyfriend at the time was a great dancer—he would often win competitions at nightclubs, so all of us women took turns getting mini-classes from him. He was a six-foot-tall black man with great moves and a smile that would melt any girl's heart.

At midnight, everyone gathered in the living room, and I put on my cousin's white dress with pink polka-dotted tulle and danced with my father to the sound of Strauss. The little child in me went to bed as happy as could be.

As part of my Cinderella complex, at fifteen, sex was still alien to me—in my mind, it could only happen with the perfect prince. Someone would come, I would fall in love, and we would be happy forever after. My best friends, Cristiane and Ana, were the opposite; they definitely had more hormones than I, which meant that they were normal teenagers, and I was the odd one out.

Cristiane and I were inseparable, and I used to regularly spend the weekend at her house. I learned and changed a lot because of her. She unveiled a much bolder and more fun world to me, where everything was relative and most rules could be broken, especially when it came to school. What attracted me to her was the fact that she was fearless—life needed to be lived with intensity, in her eyes, and that perspective was captivating.

I smoked my first cigarette with Cristiane. She also introduced me to the subject of sex, always in a caring way, never judging my weird choice of chastity or my childlike daydreams. We used to call each other Laurel and Hardy, which in Brazil was translated as "The fat and the skinny"—not that she was fat at all, but I was very thin and she was stronger than me, so we decided that made sense.

We had two passions in common: the school band, in which we both played, and pitomba, a fruit quite similar to lychee, but with less meat. Not a very popular one, because it is sour and has very little meat, but we loved it and would go to any lengths to find it. Many times, we would ride for one hour on a bus to downtown because they had the best pitombas in Recife. We would fill up our backpacks and return, eating them all the way home.

Those days were probably the times I strayed most from home. During the week, I had classes in the morning. In the afternoon, I took part in a few dance groups, went to English school, and rehearsed for band performances, which included Saturdays. Renata and Eveline were also part of the band.

My parents were very present and supportive of these extracurricular activities, particularly the marching band. They encouraged us to bring our friends home because, according to my wise mom, by having them around, she could see who we were hanging out with. Cristiane was the one friend I felt comfortable bringing home—she was so laid back and non-judgmental that I didn't care if she saw my father's drinking spurges.

She never brought the subject up. It was just not an issue; I honestly think she didn't even notice, and if she did, she was kind enough not to mention a thing. I remember envying her relationship with her father. She was clearly his favorite, and they shared so much. I looked up to them and wished I could have the same kind of relationship.

My attitude toward my father reflected how insecure I felt in his presence. Apart from the drinking, he had a short temper and would go from happy to angry in no time. His outbursts often startled and scared me, so my only option was to avoid it as much as possible, which affected my participation in everyday family rituals. Eating together was one of them; I would always find an excuse to eat by myself.

Sometimes, in an effort not to upset my dad, my mom would ask me to join them at the table. She knew why I wanted to be alone, but felt sad for him, because it broke his heart. Her pleas just added more guilt to my already-long list of self-blame. I wanted to hurt him but hated myself for doing so. I often asked myself: How can I reject a father who is present, caring, and dedicated? How is it so hard for me to accept and love him?

I don't know if this is common with alcoholics, but in my father's case, he went through phases of inebriation. At first, the alcohol would enhance his sense of humor, but that only amused others, never us, because we knew where we were heading. Then, he'd want to be the center of attention—he'd raise his voice, telling endless repetitive stories, becoming highly inconvenient. The next stage was the worst. It was as if his past came dawning over him. He would become silent, depressed, and introspective. That was the most difficult part for me to bear, because I knew he was in pain but didn't know why. After that, when he could hardly talk, he would fall asleep, only to start yet again the following day.

For all of us kids, all those phases were hard to witness. When you are a child of an alcoholic, it is as if with each sip, you lose a piece of the person you love. Little by little, my father would distance himself from us, and in the end, we were left with a stranger whose behavior was intolerable.

Although his alcohol dependence was hard on all of us, I was by far the one who reacted most openly to it. My harsh and cold demeanor toward him was one of the ways I chose to express the anger I felt at his lack of control. As is normal for a kid, my rational self just couldn't understand why, knowing that it hurt us so much, he couldn't just stop. My revenge was to ignore his presence, to spend as little time with him as I could, because I knew that being invisible to his kids hurt him deeply. There was nothing he wanted more than to be the perfect father, the one he never had.

For Renata, the escape was her room; she turned it into a personal refuge. I remember she would spend most of her time immersed in cigarette smoke, listening to hard rock and reading avidly. But although we both locked ourselves in, her personality was the opposite of mine. She has always been able to speak her mind and vent her feelings, very much like my dad. Dido was the same, and Eveline took it out on my mother—they argued a lot. She rarely ever talked about my dad's alcoholism, even in her adulthood. With time, we all made peace with it.

For me, expressing my feelings was extremely hard; I was an introvert. Silence and tears were my way to deal with it, mostly on my own. I still have trouble sharing tears in public, even with those who are close to me. At the same time, I was the daughter he danced waltz, tango and bolero with, and he was the father who cheered and supported us in all our personal choices, no questions asked. He respected us and believed that the best way to help us grow was to let us make mistakes. My brother Dido loved sports and changed modalities all his life. My father was always by his side, watching games and helping him fulfill his dreams. With Renata, they shared a love for music and books; with Eveline, well, as I've mentioned before, she was his little princess. They shared emotion.

Alcohol changed all that. I felt that I had two fathers: the sober one, whom I admired, and the one transformed by alcohol. I wanted the first and despised the second. It is natural for kids to look at their parents as role models. For me, my mother was that. She was also a martyr, a victim of a generation that forced women to stay with their drunken husbands.

She needed protection, and if I couldn't change her fate, I could at least try to make it easier for her, so I played the role of the perfect daughter. I was focused on her well-being, as if I could make up for the pain he caused us, a distorted perception of the situation for sure, but one that made sense in a child's eye.

When I look back, I see many clues as to how disruptive my relationship with my father was. The nickname he gave me—"old lady with a bun"— for example, shows how he viewed me as a strict, serious child, someone who could not accept other people's flaws. And he was right, I really couldn't. This affected not only in the way I dealt with him, but also in how I interacted with Renata and Dido.

I was highly critical of both of them, because they were a handful; they flunked at school, smoked, did drugs, and had no regard for my parent's wishes. In other words, they were typical teenagers reacting to unhealthy family dynamics. But I strived to be the opposite, always obedient, always the quiet one who never said no, and I demanded they follow my example.

In the midst of my high standards, I became detached from people. I was sweet and cuddly with a select circle of individuals, like with my cousin Roberto. He lived with us for two years in his early twenties. When writing this book, I asked him to describe me in that time. He said I was quiet and shy, but loved to snuggle. "If you trusted someone, you were very cuddly. You practically melted in my arms."

So that was me until I turned eighteen and decided to leave Brazil. I had just been accepted to college to study business and had finished my four-year English course, and I wanted to become fluent in English, so I set a plan in motion to go by myself to the United States for a year.

At the time, I worked at the place where I studied English at the front desk and as an English kindergarten teacher, so that allowed me to save some money for my trip. What I had saved in the previous two years was enough for approximately three months in the US. When I told my parents that I wanted to go, they were both very supportive, but they had no money to help me with my expenses. The only thing they could afford was the tickets, which were quite expensive then. My extended family criticized them heavily for letting me go, but they ignored everyone. I heard my dad tell one of my uncles: "I trust her."

So in 1986, with fifteen hundred dollars in my purse, I left for Dallas, where my father's friend had arranged for me to meet his son and help me get settled in. Back then, I had no idea how the following years would change me, much less the effect they would have on my relationship with my father.

Adult life

The first thought I had when I woke up in the United States, at nineteen, was "What on earth am I doing here?" Around me, a one-bathroom apartment with a tiny living room, a half-kitchen, and nothing on the walls. I was in a rough area of Dallas, Texas, living with a stranger. She was a colleague's acquaintance who agreed to share the expenses until I got a job and found my own place.

I had slept on a very uncomfortable air mattress and had no idea how I would make ends meet in that cold, flat, overwhelming city. The previous night, I'd gotten a taste of a side of Dallas I was not prepared to face. Around 8 p.m., I decided to buy some food from the supermarket across the street. Before I even got there, I was stopped by a policeman who, very worried to see a woman walking calmly around the neighborhood, said, "Do you have any idea of the risk you're taking? Go home now, and don't walk in this neighborhood again."

My English was pretty rusty but good enough to understand the danger I had naively put myself in, so I decided that my growling stomach could wait a few more hours, until the following day. I felt scared, alone, and helpless. Back at the apartment, we had no phone and no TV, and cell phones weren't around yet. I spent most of the night awake, questioning my decision to leave what I had in Brazil.

I decided to get a phone that same week, after waking up in the middle of the night to the sound of someone trying to break into the apartment. A few days later, I had another scare. The apartment was on the ground floor. Around 10 p.m., I heard someone trying to break my window, so I called the police. They came a few minutes later, and after examining the area they concluded that the front door had been tampered with and there were footprints leading to the side window. That night, once again, they advised me to leave the neighborhood as soon as possible.

Luckily, I soon got my first job as a pizza delivery person, the shortest career of my life. My total lack of sense of direction turned the deliveries into a fiasco. I would often arrive at the address on the order with a cold pizza, which meant that it would have to be comped. The owners cut me some slack at first, but two weeks into the job, after spending almost two hours lost inside an apartment complex, I was fired.

I continued working in small restaurants for a few months, going from serving at a Chinese place in a shopping mall food court to waitressing in an Italian restaurant. The experience was useful for me in terms of deciding that I would never own a restaurant myself.

Again, through people I met, I signed up for an agency specializing in underemployment for immigrants. The owner was very nice but wasn't able to find me a position. Luckily, my next job found me. One day, my friend Keila, who worked at a chocolate place in downtown Dallas, was talking to me on the phone when a customer came in and heard her talking. She asked her if she was speaking Portuguese. Keila said, "Yes! I was talking to a friend from Brazil who is looking for a job." The customer, Vicki, asked what kind of job I was searching for, and they started chatting. It just so happened that she was looking for a nanny, so they exchanged phone numbers. Days later, I was in Vicki's living room for a job interview.

Moving into that home changed my life in the United States. There, I found a compassionate, big-hearted American couple who needed a babysitter for their two children, Brett and Shawn, nine and eleven years old at the time. I would also be responsible for housekeeping, cleaning, and cooking. My connection with Vicki, Gerald and the boys was immediate. Soon, they became my family.

I am not exaggerating when I call them family, not at all. We also fought like a family. The boys and I, that is. Brett, the younger brother was sweet, affectionate, and extremely sensitive, a real sweetheart (he still is). Shawn, the older, was quite energetic and curious, a generous and somewhat naive child. But boys are boys, and I had no experience dealing with them, so we argued as siblings do. They would listen to me most of the time, but they would drive me nuts with their messy room, which I was supposed to clean every single day.

At night, after dinner, I would stay with Gerald and Vicki in the living room, talking in front of the TV. We would discuss the day, watch TV shows, and listen to Elvis Presley, Gerald's all-time favorite singer. A few months after I moved in with them, I decided to go to Eastfield College in Garland, where we lived. By then, the couple had practically adopted me as their daughter, and were helping me with everything I needed for school. They actually hired a lawyer to take care of the paperwork for adoption so that I could stay in the US, but I was too old for that.

They used to say they were proud of my determination to study. I would end up spending most of the money I made paying for school. They helped me with the rest. Every night, I would borrow Gerald's car to drive to class. His computer was the only one in the house, and I used it for my homework and studying. They also bought my books so that I could save some money. If that is not the definition of a family, I don't know what is.

After I started college, I had very little spare time for anything else. I would work during the day, go to school at night, and sleep. With time, it started taking a toll on me. I felt tired and sleep-deprived most of the time, because I had to wake up early in the morning to make sure the boys had breakfast and were ready for school. Apart from that, cleaning was a big sacrifice for me, because I really didn't like doing it. I began to feel exhausted.

When I think about those days, it's clear to me that I was experiencing a mild episode of depression. On top of that, my heart had been badly broken by a man I was in love with, which just added to the already-distressing situation. I remember going to a therapist and not being able to talk, just crying the whole session.

The moments when I felt most alone were when I fell ill. I had my American family's love, but I longed for my mother, father, and siblings back in Brazil. Renata had come to Dallas a year after I arrived, but she was in a difficult phase of her life and suffered a lot in the United States, which only added to my concerns.

My father visited us once. Dallas doesn't have much to offer in terms of entertainment, so we spent most of the time chatting. Our days together were much better than what we had in Brazil, but I never stopped worrying about his drinking. The fear of him losing control was always present. I was afraid that he would embarrass me in front of friends who knew nothing about my past and my family problems. I believe he knew that, and during the days he was with us, he never got drunk.

Being far from Brazil allowed me to examine my family dynamics in a more forgiving manner. Little by little, I was maturing, and after three-and-a-half years away from home, I was ready to go back.

The return was quite tough. Our house back home had been sold, and with it went my childhood memories. My parents had made the decision to move out after eight burglars invaded the house, taking all of their belongings. The neighborhood had changed drastically, taken over by drug-trafficking gangs. Many of our friends from the slums had been murdered.

We went to live in the suburbs in a small condo that belonged to my grandfather. The positive side was that next door to us lived our Uncle Marcelo—my mother's brother—along with his wife Celia and their three kids. It was a delight to live near them. My uncle was playful and very affectionate with all of us. He and my mother were very close. Aunt Celia, who is still around, remains my favorite aunt to this day.

When I arrived, my father was living alone in São Paulo due to a job transfer. It was one of the most difficult phases for him, because he was far from his family—my mother remained in Recife—and he hated the capital of São Paulo, with its busy and polluted streets. My flight had a layover in São Paulo, so I decided to spend the weekend with him. It was a nightmare. I was immediately exposed to what I dreaded the most: his drinking, which had escalated quite a bit by that time.

During the two days I was there, he drank non-stop. It was a dreadful wake-up call for me. The reality I had worked so hard to flee had once again hit me hard. His drinking seemed to have worsened over time. The loneliness that my father felt was palpable—he couldn't stand being away from us, so he drowned his pain in alcohol.

I could not wait to go to Recife. While in São Paulo, I had the company of my sister Eveline, who had moved there to take flying lessons. She had changed radically during my years in the United States. When I left Brazil, Eveline was a teenager who wanted to be a model. When I returned, I found a woman who was sure of herself and determined to thrive in a male-dominated world.

The life experience I gained in the United States helped me in many ways. One of them was to allow me to reflect on my distant relationship with my father and the reasons why I idealized my mom. But I still needed help. One of the first things I did, as soon as I arrived in Recife, was look for a therapist. A friend referred me to Lepê, a short, slim, black man who always wore a colored hat and adopted a very straightforward style.

In our first session, as soon as I opened the door to his office, he looked at me from a distance—he was sitting behind a small table surrounded by thousands of books—and uttered a sharp remark that made a shocking impact on me: "You must be the daughter of a military man." I asked him why he thought that, and he said, "That 'look down your nose' attitude is typical." In the midst of the anger and indignation, I decided that this was the place for me, because I felt I needed someone with that kind of attitude to shake me up.

Lepê helped me modify the way I saw our family patterns, particularly the role I played in them. Our time together was brief, albeit intense. After eight sessions of surprises and meaningful discoveries, I ended up feeling closer to my father. One of the reasons for that was that I realized how similar we were. Contrary to my strongly held belief in the opposite, his influence on me had shaped me more than my mother's. Naturally, at first, I was reluctant to admit this to myself, but Lepê guided me through the path of self-knowledge. From that point on, my relationship with Dad took a turn for the better.

The resemblance was so great that I had even adopted some of his mannerisms over the years. One day, a friend asked me why I had a habit of saluting people. I laughed, thinking it was a joke, but I started paying attention to myself, and one night, when arriving at a friend's house, instead of waving my hand to the guests, as it is the custom in Brazil, I caught myself saluting them. *Are you kidding me?* I thought. It took me months to stop doing that, it was such an ingrained habit.

In addition to seeing my dad in a more balanced light, I had to deconstruct the image I had of my mother. After therapy, I altered my perception of her as being a fragile women, realizing that she had strengths and weaknesses like anyone else. Above all, I came to terms with the fact that she was not perfect, much less a victim in a situation she could not change. I left therapy more self-aware and with a totally different picture of my family from the one I had when I started. At that time, I was preparing for the university entrance exam, still not sure about the career I wanted to pursue. The only thing I knew after studying computer science in the US was that programming was not for me. In the end, I chose Journalism. A year after coming back to Brazil, I was engaged to Mario, whom I had met at Cultura Inglesa, an English school where I worked as a teacher and in the admissions office.

We got married quickly, and just as fast, two years later, we got divorced. I remember telling my father about the decision to separate. The conversation was short, welcoming, and practical.

"Dad, I'm getting a divorce," I said.

He looked up—he was reading at the table—and asked, "Are you sure that's what you want?"

"Yes," I replied.

"Then come home. I'm by your side for whatever you need." He looked down and kept reading.

But I didn't go back. Renata and her husband, Gustavo, invited me to live with them, a warmhearted decision I will never forget, especially from Gustavo—after all, he would have to take in a sister-in-law. It was actually he who persuaded me to accept their offer. He told me about the time he had gotten divorced and how he'd dreaded the idea of going back to his parents' home. I said yes and stayed with them for two years.

When I got married, my dad was already back in Recife, and my parents had moved to an apartment in a nice neighborhood called Graças. Their marriage was not going well, and one day my father summoned us for a family talk. With a full glass in his hand, he told us that mom had asked for a divorce. Annoyed at the scene, I was once again cruel to him, and replied, "And the problem is in your hand. If I were her, I would not have been able to put up with it for so long." Stifled, he promised he would treat the addiction, but he never did.

Somehow, they overcame the crisis and remained married, but the tension between the two was visible. Only my youngest brother, Adisio, lived with them, and his presence added pain and worry to their already-fragile relationship. Dido, as we called him, had been a drug addict for many years at that point, and very much like my father, he refused to admit he had a problem.

We suffered greatly from my brother's choices. The lack of boundaries and limits he had as a child had turned into a blatant disregard for his own life. He had quickly progressed from mild to hard-core drugs. It was difficult to know what he was high on, because he used a variety of substances, never admitting he was out of control.

For my dad, besides the pain of witnessing Dido's destructive path, there was the disappointment of a father who had dreamed of a bright future for his only son. In his mind, Dido would go to college, something he himself had not personally accomplished. My brother did the opposite. He dropped out of school in the eighth grade with no plans to build a conventional career. Instead, he trained to be a parachuting instructor. Dedicated and meticulous, Dido was admired by his peers, not only as a professional but also for his laughter and his friendly demeanor. My brother was generous, affectionate, and totally detached from material things. He was also naïve and saw only the good side of people.

As was typical of my father, he supported Dido in his choices and made sure to be there for him. He immersed himself in the skydiving scene and was always present during my brother's open classes, which often happened during the weekends. During one of these classes, I came to see him, and one of his students had been a no-show, so he invited me to come with him on a tandem parachuting experience. I immediately said yes.

He suited me up, and soon we were waiting for the plane to reach the ideal altitude. I remember him telling me to step off the plane and asking, "Do you want the full experience or a safer one?" I said, "Well,

I doubt I will do this again, so give me everything you've got." He did. During the jump, he let me pilot the canopy. Looking around, I shouted, "Wow, now I get why you do this, Dido. It's incredible." That day with him was one of the most special moments we shared in our lives.

The relationship between my father and Dido was very close. They had a certain shared complicity, and even when they argued, Dido was always a patient and caring son. Unlike me, who would shut off and hurt my dad with silence, I never once saw my brother be rude to him when he was drunk, maybe because substance use was something they had in common. Whatever the reason, my brother never used it against my father.

In 1996, after taking LSD, Dido had his first psychotic episode. I was working when I got a phone call from my mother, asking me to find Dad because Dido was out of control and needed to be hospitalized. Together, my father and I went to pick him up. On the way there, I called a friend who specialized in the treatment of addiction—I knew where we needed to take him. I will never forget what I saw when we found him. Dido could not stand still. He looked at us with glassy eyes, spoke compulsively, and made no sense at all.

While we waited for the ambulance, I managed to get him to sit down for a few minutes. I made it clear to him that whether he agreed or not, he would be taken to a rehab facility. By then, my father and I had agreed on involuntary commitment, and we were prepared for the worst, but my brother promptly agreed to go. He was in treatment for thirty days of ups and downs in a small clinic in Recife.

The first days were the worst, because he was so dazed with medication that it was hard for him to even talk. There were moments when he was angry at being there and begged us to let him leave. Even at the height of his frustration, Dido never blamed us or took it out on us. He would just plea to go home. It was heartbreaking to see him like that, and even harder to stick to our decision, but we knew that the clinic was the safest place for him to be.

Every day, my father and I would visit him. Dad would come in the mornings and I in the afternoons. We alternated, because my sisters were not living in Recife anymore, and seeing my brother like that was too hard on my mom. It was just too painful for her, so she wouldn't come. Dido and I only talked about this once, when I asked him if he was angry at her for not visiting. He told me he understood why it was too much for her. One day, while we were chatting on the patio, with his head on my lap, he looked at me and said, "I will never forget what you are doing for me, Nina." (That's my family nickname.) I still get teary eyes when I think of that.

I remember the only joint family therapy session we had, which was the only time my mother came to the rehab facility. It was also the first time I saw my brother lash out at my dad for his drinking. Whatever he had been holding inside came out that day in full force. I don't recall what my dad had said prior to Dido's outburst, but I certainly will never forget his reply. "Who are you to talk about my addiction? The only difference between us is the drug we use—you're just as dependent as me." My father lowered his head in shame and remained silent for the rest of the session.

These were hard times for my dad. As much as we knew about my brother's drug addiction, no family is ever prepared to see a loved one in that situation. Gradually, Dido regained his ability to think straight, but even after the painful experience of rehab, he never expressed any intentions to become drug-free.

Shortly after my brother was discharged, I was invited to work in Brasilia, Brazil's capital. I moved there in January of 1997. From a distance, I heard about his second and third involuntary commitments, both of them with similar treatments and outcomes. At the time, Renata was back in Recife, and Eveline, who was living in São Paulo, visited him whenever she could. As for my father, he remained present and never lost hope of one day seeing his son drug-free, whole again, in complete recovery.

On July 18, 1998, his hopes were ended. A month after leaving the clinic for the third time, my brother went hang-gliding, his new passion, and forgot to bolt the equipment. The wings collapsed, and he went into free fall, dying instantly in a town near Recife.

I was visiting Eveline in São Paulo when we received the call. The only image I have of that day is of the two of us sitting in silence on the stairs outside her home. There were simply no words to be said. When her husband arrived, we rushed to the airport and boarded a flight to Recife. At the funeral, I saw my father in a state I had never seen him before. He was confused, walking around, lost in his pain. People would come up to him, and he would erratically explain the accident in detail, as if he was trying to convince himself of what had happened to his son. On that day, a piece of him was buried with my brother.

At one point I decided that he had reached his limit, so I approached my dad and asked him to go home. There was nothing more to be done. He looked at me, confused, and agreed to go. I'm not sure he even knew what he was agreeing with, but I do remember giving him a sedative before he left.

During the week I spent in Recife, I did not shed a tear. This is my usual defense mechanism when the pain is too much to bear. I took care of the telephone calls and the practical things that usually follow a funeral. Years later, my sisters told me they were worried sick about my silence and apparent calm. The worst day for me was when we emptied my brother's room. We didn't want my mother and father to have to go through that themselves. Each one of us chose something to keep. I took a pair of shorts.

While in Recife, although I did not express my pain, I had one of the worst asthma attacks of my life. I also had a fever the whole time I was there. Once I was back in my apartment in Brasilia, I collapsed in bed, crying for hours, alone. When I got up, my temperature and breathing had returned to normal.

After my brother's death, Dad diverted the love he had for him to Ícaro, Dido's only son, who was two years old and lived with his maternal grandmother in Serrambi, a beach seventy kilometers from Recife. Every weekend, Dad would visit his grandson. Having spent time with his father in the skydiving facility, Ícaro was fascinated by airplanes, so my father would buy wooden model planes for the two of them to assemble together.

Dad would teach the little boy the Brazilian Army anthem, just as he had done with Dido when he was a child. He would build him kites, take him to the beach, and play around. They become best buddies. One day, my father was informed by Ícaro's grandmother that they were moving to Sergipe, a state five-and-a-half hours from ours by car. The loss of his presence was another heavy blow to my father.

In 1999, I returned to Recife and stayed again at Renata's home. The apartment was vacant, because they were spending a year in England. In July, I moved to my own apartment. Every week, along with Renata, Gustavo and Clara (my niece, who was born in 2000), I would go to my parents' house, but the visit was never relaxing. My parent's relationship was getting worse every day; they barely talked to each other, and we were forced to divide our time between talking with Mom and Dad, alternately.

Meanwhile, my father was in a very unstable situation at work. The business conglomerate where he had been working for a few years as a supply director was about to sell the companies. With the sale came layoffs, and my father was again unemployed, this time as a man over sixty, and therefore with little chance of repositioning.
Over the next few months, his savings were fading. At the time, he had started a relationship with Sonia, a young woman who worked at a pizza place he used to go to frequently. One day, I invited him to lunch, and we

had a long and difficult conversation about his future, his marriage to my mother, and his feelings for Sonia.

Our lunch lasted the whole afternoon. I tried to show him that his daughters would be supportive if he left mom to be with the new woman. I knew he was terrified of being judged or criticized by us; he would never make the decision to leave if we were against it. Previously, I had talked to my sisters, and we had agreed on how to approach the issue with him.

During our conversation, I disclosed our discomfort at family gatherings and how much we suffered to see both of them unhappy in a marriage that had been over for years. Dad also had doubts about Sonia, particularly due to the age difference between them. I argued that she seemed to be in love with him, and it would be up to her to make such decision. "I'm not sure about any of it, Paula. What if it doesn't work?" he asked. "Dad, the only thing we all know for sure is that you and mom are unhappy together, and neither one of you deserve to go on like this, so why not try?" I replied. A week later, he left home, and within a few months moved in with Sonia, her two children, and her mother. Once again, my dad had a family, and I believed that maybe the change would renew his life and bring a new light to his future, but unfortunately, things did not go as smoothly as I had imagined.

A few months later, he invited me to lunch, saying that he needed to take care of a few practical things and needed my help. I was to bring documents. When I arrived, he asked me to sign some paperwork so that we could open a joint account. I signed everything without making much of it.

He also explained to me what should be done in case something happened to him. The apartment where my mother lived should be hers. Sonia should have the one they shared, and his retirement pension would be entirely given to my mother. He told me in detail how much he had in his savings account and which life insurances he had, making sure to say that he had no outstanding debts. He would transfer everything to our joint account so that I could withdraw the money and distribute it as planned.

Although today it may seem that he was already planning his own death, I still have a hard time believing that, because his suicide didn't occur until around three years later. Maybe, at the time we had lunch, he had planned to kill himself sooner, and for some reason changed his mind. I will never know. My dad was always overly organized and disciplined, so it didn't seem farfetched to me, everything he told me that day.

We usually met on a weekly basis. Sometimes, he would come to my apartment for lunch. He was having a lot of financial difficulties, and we would spend a lot of time trying to figure out how to solve them. I don't recall precisely why, but I began to notice that his mental health and mood were deteriorating. In the past, even when he was struggling, my father always remained optimistic, but that had markedly changed. When we met, he seemed distant, immersed in troubling thoughts that he wasn't able to share. He just didn't know how.

His condition worsened after he opened a pizzeria near the apartment where he was living with Sonia. They ran the place together, and business was not going well. I remember being in his home with him one day and Dad repeating over and over again that starting a business at his age was stupid, that he should have left the money in the savings account rather than risk it all in something he knew nothing about.

A few days later, he asked me for one more favor. I was to transfer the rest of his money to my private account, so that I could manage his finances. It wasn't much, but he felt he couldn't handle it by himself anymore. He felt fearful and insecure. Every month, without him knowing it, I would pay some of his bills so that his money could be enough for the rest of his expenses. My father was a proud man, and I knew that it would be shameful for him to have his daughter help him financially.

Meanwhile, Renata, Gustavo, Clara and I tried to cheer him up by coming to his pizza place for lunch on Sundays. When he wasn't around, we shared our concerns about him, particularly his stubbornness and his difficulty in accepting help from friends and family. He had always been forgiving with others, but self-compassion was not his forte. Having a new family added a new layer of responsibilities. My father was old-fashioned and believed in being the sole provider, which he could not do anymore.

When the depression became apparent, I asked him to see a psychiatrist. He listened to me and made an appointment with his general practitioner, who prescribed antidepressants. I saw no improvement. He promised me he was going through with his treatment, but I doubt he ever did. This is one of the hardest things for those who have a family member with a mental illness. It's hard to know for sure if they are taking their medication.

In 2004, my father decided to close the restaurant. I was away on vacation when this process began, so I followed very little of it. What I do know is that he telephoned Uncle Sobrinho, asking him to locate the landlord and to try to persuade her not to charge the fine stipulated in the contract. I was in Miami and planned to stay there for two months, returning in early January 2005. We talked on the phone a few times while I was there, and he seemed better. Today, I know that this is one of the most common warning signs given by a suicidal person. They seem to have regained joy for life while planning their own death (see the explanation of this in the Warning Signs chapter).

On Sunday, January 9, I called Renata to find out how things were going. She told me that Dad would come soon to spend the afternoon with her and Clara. While we were still on the phone, he arrived, and she asked me if I wanted to chat with him. I said I would call him later in the week. It took me years to get over the guilt of not talking to him on the last day of his life.

All afternoon, Renata sensed that something was wrong with my father. She couldn't pinpoint what, but there was something off. More than once, she sensed that he was about to cry. His lips would shake, and his eyes would fill up with tears for no apparent reason. The idea of him contemplating suicide did occur to her, but she couldn't utter the words. As soon as he left, she called me, worried, not knowing what to do. She was sure Dad had given up on life. I tried to calm her down by saying that I would be back in three days and we would talk before then, but little did I know that I had no time left. The following morning, I got the second-hardest call of my life.

CHAPTER TWO

What is Suicide?

Suicide is a ubiquitous word nowadays. It has become so common that some reflection on its meaning is necessary, especially in terms of when to apply the word to a particular death. At first glance, it may seem like a simple task to rule a particular death as being self-inflicted, but in many cases, there's much room for interpretation. Throughout history, philosophers, coroners, doctors, and free thinkers have tried to reach a clear and objective definition of the word itself. Such discussions remain energized to this day, and they generate a debate as complex as the theme itself. At the heart of this heated discussion lies the matter of intent.

In certain situations, the circumstances of death leave no room for doubt. A person who has shown signs of an unfulfilled life, made use of a violent method—such as a firearm—and left a farewell note giving reasons for killing themselves raises no questions as to their goal. Another example is someone who organizes their finances and prepares their yearly income tax prior to death. Not everyone leaves such clear clues, however. There are several scenarios where it might be hard to conclude what really happened. In some cases, certainty will never be reached. I personally witnessed one of these cases.

Roberto was the oldest brother of a close friend of mine. Outwardly, he led a balanced life with a wife, three small kids, sound financial status, good health, and a successful career. At the end of 2006, he was found dead after falling into a gap in his building's plumbing system As the analysis of his death began, facts were called into question regarding its seemingly accidental nature.

I was with my friend when he received the news about his brother. He immediately went to check the site and soon realized that there was no way an adult could have fallen into that gap by accident, as it was surrounded by a protective wall. The family began to suspect suicide. Roberto had arrived late that night and was home alone when he died. One of the theories was that maybe he had been drinking, which could have led him to slip through the open space, but suppositions like this were quickly dismissed, as he was not a habitual drinker, and no empty bottles were found anywhere in the vicinity.

Homicide was also out of the question, because nobody else had entered the building that night. What led the family to suspect intentional death, then? Around two years prior to his death, Roberto had experienced a panic attack while he was abroad. At the time, he spent hours in his hotel bed, in a semi-catatonic state. His friends had to help him calm down and keep him company until he was able to return to Brazil. As far as everyone knows, Roberto sought medical help, but he didn't go through with the prescribed treatment, so maybe he had experienced another panic attack and, in an act of desperation, thrown himself into the gap. To this day, no one knows exactly what happened.

This case exemplifies one of the dilemmas regarding intent in relation to self-inflicted death. Was Roberto well aware of what he was doing, or was it only an act of someone who had momentarily lost control? If so, could we attest without a doubt that he had died by suicide? As we can see, the ambivalence that is characteristic of self-inflicted deaths outlives the act itself, because in many instances, we cannot reach definite conclusions.

The word suicide comes from Latin, from the roots *sui* (of oneself) and *caedes* (the action of killing)—in other words, "to kill oneself." The first dictionary to define it was the Oxford English Dictionary, in 1661, and it took a full century for others to follow suit. Notice how some of them would rather use vague explanations, while others detail the action specifically:

Oxford English Dictionary – The action of killing oneself deliberately. Webster English Dictionary – The act or an instance of taking one's own life voluntarily and intentionally.

In his book *Man Against Himself,* the American psychiatrist Karl Menninger posits that suicide involves three internal elements: the desires to die, to kill, and to be killed. Therefore, it's inherently an act where the subject is, at the same time, victim and perpetrator. One important consideration should also be considered: whether or not the act was intentional and voluntary. Sometimes, this question is never answered, which adds additional distress and lack of closure to those left behind.

Adriana, whom I interviewed for this book, attempted suicide amidst a psychotic episode in which she heard voices telling her to hang herself. When we talked, it was clear that she had few memories of that day. Adriana had been at the peak of symptoms caused by her recently diagnosed schizophrenia, so her attempt was a result of the typical hallucinations that accompany the disease. In her case, there was no way to allege that there was indeed any intention behind her self-harm, nor can we attest that it was a voluntary act.

When we examine this theme further, additional questions arise. Child suicide is one of them. As in the case of people with mental illnesses, it is difficult to substantiate intent. In a child, full awareness of the irreversibility of death is only acquired around ten years of age, and their process for understanding their own actions is unsophisticated. The prefrontal cortex—an area of the brain responsible, among other things, for decision-making—is not fully developed until an individual reaches around 25 years of age. This directly impacts a child's comprehension of what they are doing when attempting to end their own life.

One of the people I interviewed, the Iranian woman called Mahnaz, illustrates well the poor judgment she exhibited when she took approximately two hundred pills after an argument with her stepmother. She was twelve at the time:

"I became the trouble girl. I'd run away from home; he would find out and beat me up. I couldn't care less—the emotional pain was so deep that I simply stopped caring. During a fight with my step-mother, I went into the medicine cabinet and took everything I could find. I swallowed almost two hundred pills at the time.

While I was doing that, I thought, "I'll show you." That was my only thought then, to teach them a lesson. I actually wanted to be saved; maybe the new woman would be blamed for everything, and then she would have to go away, and life would go back to normal. I woke up at the hospital after being unconscious for two days. I was lucky to have survived."

Mahnaz' intended motivation was to punish her father and stepmother for the pain and suffering they'd put her through. She told me she never wanted to die and never thought about the consequences she would have to face if she survived. She was looking to go back to life as she knew it, no matter how complicated it was.

Compared to what she was living through at the time, the fights between her father and mother seemed a better option than being away from her mother and sharing her father's love with a sister she refused to acknowledge. This is another case where intent to die is not easily identifiable; it was not her primary goal, or even her goal at all, and consequently, it would be incorrect to characterize the attempt as a voluntary act, at least regarding the intention to cease living.

Unconscious impulses

Beyond defining suicide per se, it is also important to reflect on a different type of behavior. While some people never really contemplate taking their own life, they might present self-destructive behaviors that could easily lead to death. Karl Menninger defined three types of suicide. The first is the chronic type, which includes alcoholism, martyrdom and asceticism.

The second is the focal suicide: self-mutilation and accidents that are psychologically motivated, even if unconsciously. Regarding self-mutilation, in the "Youth and Suicide" chapter, I'll explore non-suicidal self-injury (NSSI), a concept which expands Menninger's view considerably, especially within the context of youth.

The last type of suicide is organic, involving psychological factors associated with various illnesses. According to Menninger, these behaviors subtly contribute to patterns individuals engage in that shorten or limit their lives.

When it comes to unconscious impulses, another factor comes to mind, one that has accompanied me throughout my life: people who are always involved in life-threatening activities. They are commonly seen as free-spirited, fearless individuals who enjoy life intensely. Of course, such classifications must be used with care so as not to seem overly judgmental. There is nothing wrong with being adventurous. A mountain-climbing aficionado is not necessarily suicidal. In order to examine this from a perspective of self-harm, one needs to observe broader aspects of the person's life: patterns of behavior, outlook on life, daily activities, strength of relationships, family mental health history, stressors, emotional state, etc.

In some cases, however, to distinguish between someone who explores a wide spectrum of experiences from one who indulges in self-destructive acts is somewhat straightforward. My brother was like that. Early on in life, he often opted for the extremes. He wasn't happy to just ride his bike; he had to jump over obstacles with it. He switched from sport to sport, each riskier than the last, ending up at skydiving, which he eventually took up professionally.

Again, being a skydiving instructor doesn't necessarily mean following a path of self-destruction; most people who opt for this profession are extremely careful, and my brother was known for his high standards of safety. He was also athletic and hardly ever felt threatened— his threshold was quite high when it came to fear. But that was not the full story. The constant quest for a boost of adrenaline included drug use, which started when he was thirteen and escalated dangerously until, by his early twenties, it was significantly affecting my brother's mental health.

At twenty-five, he suffered his first psychotic episode, provoked by a dose of LSD. Over the course of approximately fourteen months, he went through three rehabilitation treatments. With his skydiving license suspended, he took up hang gliding. In July 1987, he launched from a cliff and the wing closed shut, which caused him to free-fall to his death. We never found out what happened, but the general suspicion was that he had failed to assemble his glider properly.

I personally have a hard time separating his death from his drug use. It seems likely to me that he was high on something when he prepared and jumped. I will never know for certain whether that is true or not, but it is a good example of the importance of looking at an individual's life history in search of the presence of self-destructive tendencies.

When discussing self-destruction, there is a broad scope of paradigms. The American psychologist Norman Farberow, who together with psychiatrist Robert E. Litman and Edwin Shneidman founded the Los Angeles Suicide Prevention Center in 1958, posits that there are two ways in which people indirectly use a preexisting condition to engage in self-harm. For instance, someone suffering from diabetes might insist on the excessive consumption of sugary drinks, carbohydrates, and other harmful food, as a consequence hastening the progression of the disease. Similarly, when hypertensive people ingest excessive amounts of salty foods, smoke, and don't exercise, this leads to otherwise-preventable complications. Excessive eating, drinking and smoking, avoiding medical care, and drug abuse are frequently observable in our society. In chapter 5, I will explore some of these elements individually, as they are strongly linked to suicide.

Associated emotions and motivations

One of the most influential texts on the nature of a suicidal mind was written by the father of psychoanalysis, Sigmund Freud, in 1917. *In Mourning and Melancholia*, he describes the internal processes that lead an individual to self-destruction. At the center of the act is hostility aimed at people we love but who are also beyond our reach. The target of that hostility may have died or simply left us, and therefore is seen as an object of loss. Suicide would be hatred turned against oneself, murder internalized, self-punishment. For Freud, however, this is just an indirect vehicle of vengeance against the one we cannot reach any more:

"We have long known, it is true, that no neurotic harbors thoughts of

suicide which he has not turned back upon himself from murderous impulses against others . . . The analysis of melancholia now shows that the ego can kill itself only if, owing to the return of the object-cathexis, it can treat itself as an object—if it is able to direct against itself the hostility which relates to an object and which represents the ego's original reaction to objects in the external world."

Freud highlights hatred as a central element present in the suicidal act. Psychiatrists Yuan Wang and Zacaria Ramadam, in *Suicide: Fundamental Studies*, confirm Freud's theory, going as far as emphasizing that the mind of the suicidal individual sees self-destruction as a rational choice:

"Even though the person may be ambivalent, a feature of the suicidal one is turning murderous impulses (desires, needs) which have been directed against a traumatic event against themselves, even more frequently against someone who has rejected them. Suicide can be seen as murder inverted by 180 degrees."

During the interviews for this book, I asked several psychoanalysts about their impressions regarding the feelings they thought were present in self-inflicted deaths. Dr. Geraldo Massaro posed an intriguing question:

"When a person kills himself, we are all focusing about who died, but we are not used to thinking of the individual who killed. In general lines, we can see suicide as a story in which one person kills another. They internalize an external struggle— which can be against parents, for instance—that leads them to kill someone.

Is there a death? Then someone kills.

The majority of patients I have monitored had this aspect inside, generally connected to a very strong anger, sometimes originating from disappointments. This rage generates destructive actions, which turns them into omnipotent beings. Below the surface, we find frustration, disappointment, devaluing.

In several instances, insecurity deriving from lack of self-worth boosts [impulses toward] suicide. It also comes from not feeling sure of one's identity. The individual cannot help but feel his life experience has been a failure."

In *Man Against Himself*, Karl Menninger posits that the suicidal person has three main wishes: dying, killing, and being killed. Dr. Massaro's opinion that very little is said of the one who killed makes sense and is perfectly understandable. It sounds harsh, of course, to address the issue from this point of view. There is too much pain involved, and death takes a center stage after loss. This is a controversial issue among mental health professionals. Psychoanalyst Dr. Antônio Carlos Garcia, whom I interviewed, disagrees that suicide conveys a wish to kill an individual.

"Self-aggression can also be a symbolic component—the attack may be directed inward, not externally. The notion of sin, for instance. Sin can protect one from suicide as much as it can lead a person to do it. Depressed individuals sometimes believe they are great sinners and want to obliterate themselves because of that. Therefore, although every suicide involves someone doing the killing, that doesn't mean that he is a murderer. He may just want to be transformed."

Furthermore, Garcia cites love as a feeling that may also be part of the suicidal process:

"The Christian suicide, for instance, is not an act of anger, but an act of love (of an ideal), which is exactly the opposite (of anger)."

Love for one another appears as a propelling drive in what sociologist Émile Durkheim named "altruistic suicide," which is carried out for the good of the community. According to him, this happens when the person is enmeshed with their society, thus placing lower value on the individual, on themselves, and seeing the act as beneficial to the social order.

CHAPTER THREE

Global Panorama

Suicide death has been increasingly regarded as a global public health problem. The World Health Organization (WHO) estimates that approximately 800,000 people die by self-inflicted death every year, which represents one person every forty seconds[1]. One-third of the victims are young; it is the second-leading cause of death among 15- to 29-year-olds. The numbers are high, but they do not mirror the reality that goes grossly underreported by countries that do not have efficient tracking systems or societies that either criminalize or stigmatize suicide. For each self-inflicted death, WHO calculates that there are approximately twenty attempts.

Global statistics have been monitored annually by WHO since their inception in 1948, but given that the institution depends on voluntary sharing of data, the information is far from reliable. Of the 172 member states, WHO estimates that only 60 have good-quality registration of suicide. More importantly, the remaining 112 are estimated to account for 71 percent of all global self-inflicted deaths.

Several factors compound this problem. Compiling such numbers involves multileveled layers of governmental bodies, cultural elements and various medical and legal concerns. These are some of the caveats to be taken into account when analyzing the numbers presented in this chapter. It also needs to be pointed out that such data scenario has been improving. In 1950, a mere 21 countries reported their suicide rates. The quality of the tracking systems is on the rise as well, partly due to initiatives taken by WHO and the rising global awareness around suicide over the last few years.

Most of the statistics mentioned in the following pages have been extracted from the WHO's website for the year 2016, with the exception of the USA, the United Kingdom, and Australia, whose data is more recent because these countries update it regularly online. Again, the reliability of such statistics is an aspect that must never be regarded as absolute, particularly when drawing comparisons. The three aforementioned countries are among the most rigorous when it comes to notifying of deaths by suicide—and they are also the most advanced when it comes to prevention strategies—but even so, specialists believe that there is underreporting in all corners of the globe.

According to WHO, the most common misclassifications of suicide are: "death of undetermined intent," "accident," "homicide," and "unknown causes." In the Brazilian classification system, for instance, self-inflicted death belongs to the "External Causes" category, which includes deaths caused by violence and accidents. Due to incorrect reporting, it is estimated that our death logs are two to ten times smaller than what is publicly disclosed. As mentioned before, this is not just a Brazilian phenomenon. Inaccuracy is widespread.

Apart from official misclassification of voluntary death, there are several reasons why data collection is difficult. Prejudice and stigma stand out. Very frequently, families plead for suicide to not be mentioned on death certificates, either because they are embarrassed by it, or for more practical reasons, such as concern that life insurance companies will not pay benefits in cases of suicide. This is the case in many countries. Another common occurrence is the fact that on death certificates, coroners usually state the nature of the wound, not the underlying cause or intent. A shot to the heart, for example, may be related to an accident, a homicide, or self-inflicted death.

One more aspect should be mentioned. Some countries outlaw suicide, with penalties that vary from fines to life in prison, which is the case in the Bahamas, for instance. In an article published in the *International Journal of Law and Psychiatry*, in 2016, Brian Mishara, director for the Center for Research and Intervention on Suicide and Euthanasia, in Montreal, Canada, and David Weisstub, professor of Legal Psychiatry at the University of Montreal, found that twenty-five countries and states consider self-inflicted death illegal. Twenty follow Islamic or Sharia law, which usually means jail time for those who attempt to kill themselves. Encouraging or aiding someone to take their own lives is often criminalized as well. The authors analyzed criminal codes from 192 localities (see table 1).

Table 1

Countries where suicide is illegal

Source: Mishara, B., & Weisstub, D. (2016)

Country	Crime/Sentence if suicide is attempted
Bahamas	Imprisonment for life.
Bangladesh	Simple imprisonment for one or more years, or penalty of a fine, or both.
Brunei	Simple imprisonment for one or more years, or penalty of a fine, or both.

Cyprus	The offender is guilty of a misdemeanor.
Ghana	The offender is guilty of a misdemeanor.
Guyana	The offender is guilty of a misdemeanor and liable to imprisonment for two years.
India*	Simple imprisonment for one or more years, or penalty of a fine, or both.
Kenya	The offender is guilty of a misdemeanor.
Lebanon	Imprisonment.
Malawi	The offender is guilty of a misdemeanor.
Malaysia	Simple imprisonment for one or more years, or penalty of a fine, or both.
Myanmar	Simple imprisonment for one or more years, or penalty of a fine, or both.
Nigeria	The offender is guilty of a misdemeanor, and is liable to imprisonment for one year.
Pakistan	Simple imprisonment for one or more years, or penalty of a fine, or both.
Papua New Guinea	The offender is guilty of a misdemeanor, and is liable to imprisonment for one year.
Qatar	Imprisonment for up to six months and penalty of a fine of up to 3,000 riyals, or one of these two penalties.

Saint Lucia	Suicide: Aiding and Abetting of Suicide, Attempt to Commit Suicide: imprisonment for two years.
Singapore	The offender is guilty of a misdemeanor, and is liable to imprisonment for one year. Exception 5 - Culpable Homicide is not considered as a murder. Where the person who commits the suicide is above the age of eighteen years old and suffers death or takes the risk of death with their own consent.
South Soudan	The offender is guilty of a misdemeanor, and is liable to imprisonment for one year
United Republic of Tanzania	The offender is guilty of a misdemeanor.
Sudan	The offender is guilty of a misdemeanor, and is liable to imprisonment for one year.
Tonga	Imprisonment for three years.
Uganda	The offender is guilty of a misdemeanor.

*In December 2014, the Indian government announced that Section 309 of the Penal Code would be deleted.

Apart from the World Health Organization, additional data used throughout this chapter came from the Global Burden of Disease 2016 report. All data is reported considering the number of suicides per 100,000, which is the official way to measure suicide globally.

Most-affected areas

When looking at regions of the globe, the highest suicide rates are found in countries located in Southeast Asia, Europe, and Africa (see Table 2). In Southeast Asia, Thailand, Myanmar, and Singapore are at the top of the list (see Table 3). Across the world, the top rate, with 30.2 voluntary deaths per 100,000 inhabitants, is found in Guyana, in South America, followed by Lesotho (28.9), the Russian Federation (26.5), Lithuania (25.7), Suriname (23.2), Ivory Coast (23.0), Kazakhstan (22.8), Equatorial Guinea (22.0), Belarus (21.4), and the Republic of Korea (20.2). All of these are well above the global rate, which is 10.53 per 100,000 inhabitants.

Table 2

Age-Standardized Suicide Rates/Both Sexes per 100,000 Population (Regions)
World Health Organization (2016)

Region	Suicide rate
South-East Asia	13.40
Europe	12.85
Africa	11.96
Americas	9.25
Western Pacific	8.45
Eastern Mediterranean	4.30
(WHO) Global	10.53

Table 3

Suicide Rates in Southeast Asia - WHO
(Data unavailable for Laos and Brunei)

Country	2016	2015	2010	2000
Cambodia	5.9	5.9	6.3	7.3
Indonesia	3.7	3.7	4	4.3
Malaysia	6.2	6.1	6.3	7.4
Myanmar	8.1	8	7.9	7.9
Philippines	3.7	3.8	4	3.1
Singapore	7.9	7.6	8.4	11.7
Thailand	12.9	13.1	13	15.9
Timor-Leste	6.4	6.4	7.6	13.6
Vietnam	7	7	7.1	7.5

There are many factors associated with suicide, including socioeconomic, individual, biological, and cultural components. When looking at the ten countries with the highest registered rates in 2016, it seems to be no coincidence that the first two face dire economic challenges. Guyana is one of the poorest countries in South America. Lesotho, a small kingdom encircled by South Africa, is mostly rural, with few economic resources. Approximately 85 percent of the goods it consumes come from South Africa. But that number is just a narrow snapshot of their local reality; many other aspects may play a part in positioning them near the top of the list.

Three of these top countries share a common history: The Russian Federation, Belarus, and Lithuania, in third, fourth and ninth places, respectively. They all underwent socioeconomic turmoil after the collapse of the Soviet Union in 1991, which had a dramatic impact on these populations. One of the direct consequences was an increase in alcohol consumption, a known risk factor associated with suicide.

In 2015, psychiatrist Dr. Yury Razvodovsky, who specializes in addiction at Grodno State Medical University in Belarus, conducted a study[2] analyzing the correlation between alcohol sales and suicide rates in Russia and Belarus during two periods: from 1970 to 1999 and from 2000 to 2014. The results were staggering. His research suggested that each additional liter of alcohol sold per capita could increase the suicide rates by 5.0 percent in Russia and 6.1 percent in Belarus.

Dr. Razvodovsky correlates the fluctuation in the number of voluntary deaths in these two countries with other regional factors, particularly financial instability, but in the end, he posits that 55.3 percent of all suicide deaths in Russia and 56.1 percent of all suicide deaths in Belarus may be attributed to alcohol. It is interesting to note that when you compare global alcohol consumption and suicide rates, a close relationship can be observed between these two components. This doesn't mean direct causation, though. Substance abuse is often a response to stress-related factors, but whether causal or correlative, it serves as a red flag when it comes to self-inflicted death.

When looking at the Our World Data database, based at the University of Oxford, the countries featuring the highest yearly consumption[3] intersect with the suicide rate listed by the World Health Organization. Our World Data calculates their rates in liters of pure alcohol intake by individuals who are fifteen years old and older, in 2015. The total amount goes from zero to eighteen liters. Again, together with Moldova, Belarus, Lithuania, and Russia lead the ranking with highest consumptions in the world, which matches the world suicide rates published by WHO (see table 4).

Table 4

Alcohol Consumption (liters per capita, ages 15+)
Source: Our World Data, 2015

Country	Consumption
Moldova	17.4
Belarus	17.1
Lithuania	16.2
Russia	14.5
Czech Republic	14.1
Romania	12.9
Serbia	12.9
Australia	12.6
Portugal	12.5
Slovakia	12.5

Global numbers are dropping

Not all the news around suicide is bad though. Despite the overwhelming global impact of suicide, within the past three decades, the number of self-inflicted deaths has been dropping. The Institute for Health Metrics and Evaluation, IHME, based at the University of Washington, in Seattle, published a report with global numbers using the Global Burden of Disease's database, an initiative that tracks all known causes of death in 195 countries and territories—slightly more than the scope covered by WHO. They concluded that when adjusted for age and population size, although the total number of deaths by suicide increased by 6.7 percent from 1990 to 2016, the age-standardized mortality rates fell from 16.6 to 11.2 deaths per 100,000 people, a significant drop of 32.7 percent.

The IHME, which is partly funded by the Bill and Melinda Gates Foundation, excludes statistics from countries that do not have extensive registration coverage. It also tries to correct misclassification and under-reporting by reassigning codes used by the International Statistical Classification of Diseases and Related Health Problems, ICD, published by WHO. The ICD is currently the international golden standard for reporting diseases worldwide. Their report aims to identify patterns of mortality across countries using the estimates of the 2016 Global Burden of Disease.

According to the Global Burden of Disease, there were 817,000 deaths in 2016, more than the 793,000 estimated by WHO. The gender trend is similar in both sets of data, with men presenting a higher likelihood of taking their own lives than women in all regions. The only exception is the age group from fifteen to nineteen. Globally, male rates reached 15.6 deaths per 100,000, compared with 7.0 for women.[4] Suicide was the leading cause of years of life lost in the high-income Asia Pacific and was positioned within the top-ten leading causes in Eastern, Central, and Western Europe, Central Asia, Australasia, Southern Latin America, and high-income North America.

United States, Australia and The United Kingdom

These three countries are highlighted because they all have reliable data and world-recognized efforts toward suicide prevention. In the United States, suicide rates have been rising steadily over the years. From 1999 to 2017, there was a 33-percent increase in the number of deaths by suicide, going from 10.5 (29,199) to 14.0 (47,173) per 100,000 over that time period (see table 6). Females were particularly affected from 1999 to 2017 in the following age groups: 10-14 (0.5 to 1.7, respectively), 15-24 (3.0 to 5.8), 25-44 (5.5 to 7.8), 45-64 (6.0 to 9.7), and 65-74 (4.1 to 6.2). The rates in rural areas were 1.8 times higher than in most urban counties (11.1 to 20.0, respectively, per 100,000).

Since 2008, suicide has been the tenth-leading cause of death in the USA. For the 10-34 age group, it has been the second leading cause since 2016, and the fourth for ages 35-54. The most significant percentage growth has occurred since 2006. From 1999 to 2006, rates grew on average by about 1 percent per year, then by 2 percent per year through 2017. For females, the gain has been an astonishing 53 percent, from 4.0 in 1999 to 6.1 in 2017. For males, it went up 26 percent, from 17.8 in 1999 to 22.4 in 2017.

Table 6

Age-Adjusted Suicide Rates, by Sex: United States
Source: Center for Disease Control, CDC.

Year	Total Number	Rate Deaths per 100,000	Male Number	Rate Deaths per 100,000	Female Number	Rate Deaths per 100,000
1999	29,199	10.5	23,458	17.8	5,741	4.0
2000	29,350	10.4	23,618	17.7	5,732	4.0
2005	32,637	10.9	25,907	18.1	6,730	4.4
2010	38,364	12.1	30,227	19.8	8,087	5.0
2015	44,193	13.3	33,994	21.1	10,199	6.0
2017	47,173	14.0	36,782	22.4	10,391	6.1

US Male Suicide Rates (by age group)

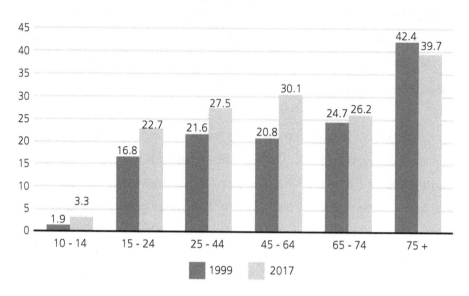

US Female Suicide Rates (by age group)

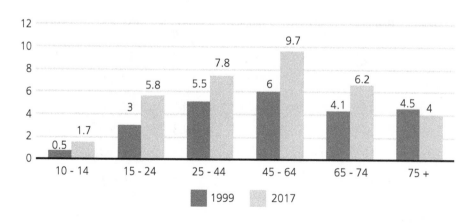

Australia

In Australia, the scenario is also worrisome. According to the country's Bureau of Statistics[5], 2017 had 9.1 percent more deaths by suicide than the previous year, with a total of 3,128. The 12.6 rate is the same as in 2015, and these are the highest recorded in the past ten years. In 2017, suicide was the thirteenth-leading cause of death in that country, moving up from the fifteenth position in 2016. Again, men, with a rate of 19.1 per 100,000, are the majority and accounted for 75.1 percent of the cases. For females, the rate is 6.2.

Australia Suicide Rates 2017 (age/sex)
Source: Australian Bureau of Statistics

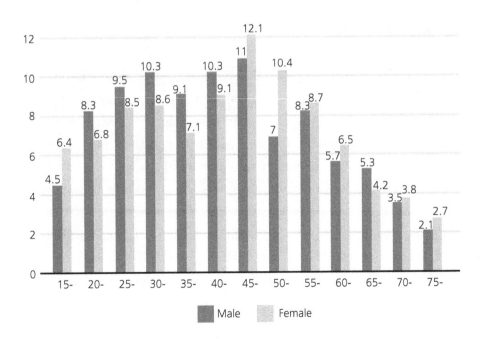

Australia Suicide Rates 2008-2017

Source: Australian Bureau of Statistics

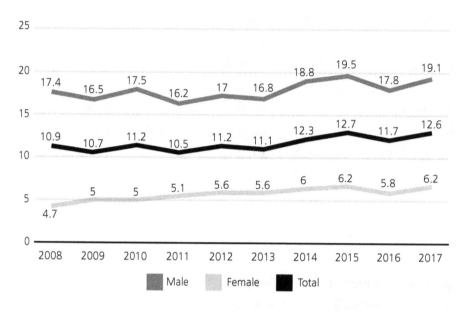

The United Kingdom

In the United Kingdom, the statistics show promising trends. In 2017, the Office for National Statistics[6] registered 5,821 deaths, a suicide rate of 10.1. For males (15.5), it was the lowest since their time series began, in 1981. For females, the rates have been consistent (4.9) across the last decade. Three-quarters of the cases in 2017 (4,382) were male, a ratio that has been constant since the mid-90s. For this population, the most affected age group has been 45-49 (24.8); for females, it's 50-54 (6.8). When looking at the countries that make up the United Kingdom, Scotland has the highest rate, with 13.9 deaths per 100,000, and England the lowest, with 9.2. Northern Ireland was not included in the numbers.

United Kingdom Suicide Rates (1981-2017)

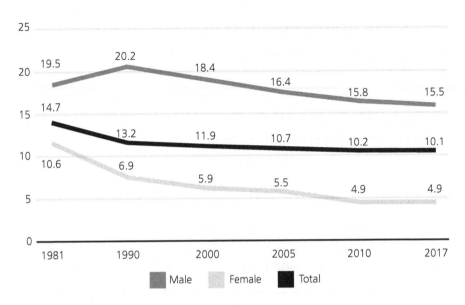

United Kingdom Suicide Rates (1981-2017) by Country

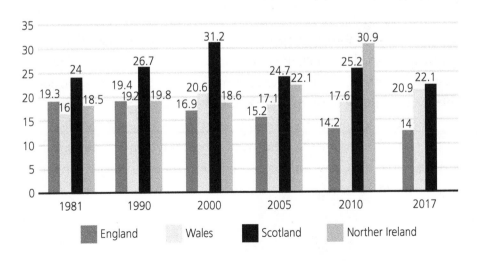

Gender differences/methods

Suicide rates reach their peak in individuals ages seventy years and over, for both men and women, in the majority of the regions in the world. In some countries, young women and men do rank higher. Globally, suicide is the second-leading cause of death in 15- to 29-year-olds. The ingestion of pesticide, hanging, and the use firearms are among the most common methods worldwide; the choice of method often varies according to the population group.

When looking at the relationship between gender and suicide, caution is paramount because, at first glance, the numbers give a false impression that suicide is a male phenomenon, which is far from true. According to WHO, the male-female world ratio of age-standardized rates in 2016 was 1.8, but this is just a superficial snapshot that leaves crucial considerations aside. The rates are different across the globe, but in general terms, women attempt suicide at two to four times the rate of men, but men die in larger numbers. In high-income countries, they die three times more than women. Low- and middle-income countries present a much lower disparity, at 1.5 men for each woman. Globally, 50 percent of all violent deaths in men are suicides. For women, the percentage is 71 percent.

The reason why more men die voluntarily has to do with the lethality of the methods used. Overall, the most common ways to die by suicide are pesticide ingestion, hanging, and firearms. Cultural factors play a major role in determining these specific trends. Poisoning by pesticides ranks high in rural agricultural areas of low- and middle-income countries. In the United States, on the other hand, where the right to bear arms is guaranteed by the Constitution's Second Amendment, firearms top the list, as seen in Table 5.

Table 5

Suicide Methods in the USA (2016)
Source: National Institute of Mental Health

Suicide Method	Number of Deaths
Total	44,965
Firearm	22,963
Suffocation	1,642
Poisoning	6,698
Other	3,662

Some hypotheses have been considered to account for the difference between male and female suicide methods. Two of them deserve note regarding the female population: easy access to medication and the misguided perception that overdose is painless. For men, the stigma of "failure" in the attempt is also slightly more significant than it is for women. Another aspect associated with females is the issue of physical appearance. They tend to choose methods that will not disfigure their bodies, particularly their face, which usually rules out the use of firearms. It may be equally an indication that they do not actually want to die, says psychoanalyst Antônio Carlos Garcia:

"This idea that beauty must be preserved above all shows that the individual does not actually want to die—they want to become something more spiritualized.

They wish to be seen for personal aspects that are currently not recognized in them.

These are all hypotheses, though, because symbols can have a million different meanings, but it only goes to show that there is always a symbolic element to suicide.

It is not simply about willingness to die, but also the desire of being transformed into something else with parts being preserved."

Garcia believes that the social role played by women influences their choices:

> *"I believe that women attempt suicide by taking pills because it is a passive way to die. They feel that they will swallow the medication, fall asleep, and feel nothing. Women do not take actions such as jumping, shooting or burning themselves. This can be related to their capacity to strongly connect with their biologic passivity and receptivity."*

On the other hand, the Psychiatry Professor for the Medicine School at Johns Hopkins University in the USA, Kay Jamison[7], argues that the perception of lethality in the method is a vital element in the choice of how to take away one's life, regardless of gender:

> *"The perception of an act's deadliness is clearly crucial to decision making. Some methods of suicide, such as jumping, hanging, or gunshot, leave little or no chance for detection or rescue by others. Nor do they allow the opportunity to change one's mind."*

When considering this issue individually, the method of choice can also be associated with the reasons each person had for taking their own life. When someone kills themself with the objective of vengeance, for instance, the concern about causing pain to others will hardly be present. Quite the contrary, in fact. In *Night Falls Fast: Understanding Suicide*, Kay Jamison talks about the connection between method and motivation:

> *"Some individuals avoid a particular suicide method because of concern about risking the lives or psychological well-being of others: they will not use carbon monoxide poisoning, for example, because gas may seep into places where other people live; cyanide, because traces of it on the lips may endanger would-be rescuers who use mouth-to-mouth resuscitation techniques; jumping, for fear of landing on other people; and gunshot or jumping because of the traumatic visual effects on survivors."*

Personality traits also play a part in this matter. In his book Suicide, published in 1897, Émile Durkheim, one of the pioneers in sociology, mentioned that each individual suicide conveys a personal message and expresses particular traits of the person, particularly their temperament, and the situation they are in; therefore, it cannot be explained only by social causes.

Following the same line of thought, an individual who tends to be more analytical and prone to planning may have a predisposition to ponder on different choices and opt for the one that better suits their needs. This seems to have been the case for Japanese writer Ryunosuke Akutagawa, who overdosed on Veronal when he was only thirty-five. In his late years, Akutagawa had been suffering from hallucinations. In his suicide note, he explained all the process of choosing how he was going to take his own life:

"My primary concern was how to die in such a way as to minimize suffering. Hanging is, of course, the most appropriate method for this purpose. But when I lingered on the image of my own dangling form, I was overcome by a lavish feeling of aesthetic disgust . . . Drowning, too, could in no way achieve my goal . . . Even in the unlikely event that I succeeded, it would prove more painful than hanging. The thought of throwing myself beneath a train evoked in me more than anything that sense of aesthetic revulsion. Death by a pistol or a knife held the potential for failure due to the trembling of my hands.

Leaping from a building would no doubt be unsightly. Based on these considerations, I settled upon death brought on by a drug. It is possible that death by a drug may be more painful than hanging. However, aside from the fact that I find it less abhorrent than hanging, it also holds the benefit that there is no danger of resuscitation.

There only remained the issue that procuring such a drug would be, needless to say, no simple task for me. I set myself upon suicide and resolved to use every means at my disposal to acquire the drug. At the same time, I tried to gain what knowledge I could of toxicology.

> *My thoughts then turned to where I would take my life. My family would have to rely on my inheritance after my death . . . I was anxious about my house becoming unmarketable because of my suicide . . ."* [8]

A final factor should be mentioned: media coverage. The wide publicity of places commonly used for suicide, such as the Golden Gate Bridge in San Francisco, USA, for instance, may stimulate contagion, a widely researched phenomenon in suicidology. Both themes—method and media coverage—are mentioned by the World Health Organization when addressing prevention. WHO recommends restricting access to methods as one of the main actions to be taken for prevention. The other steps highlighted are:

- Responsible reporting by the media.
- Alcohol policies to lower harmful use.
- Early identification, treatment, and care for people with mental illness, substance use disorders, chronic pain, and emotional distress.
- Health worker training (non-specialized) in the assessment and management of suicidal behavior.
- Follow-up care for those who attempted suicide.

Cultural factors

Religion

Among the cultural factors that play a role in how suicide is perceived, religion deserves a closer examination. Most major organized religions have condemned it based on the belief that only God gives us life and only He can take it from us. In Jewish law, although suicide is forbidden, contemporary rabbis tend to differentiate individuals who take their lives as a result of mental illness, in which case they are allowed to have traditional burials. Only the named lada'at—a person of sound mind—is seen as going against the Law by completing suicide[9].

A similar view occurs in Christianity. According to the Catechism of the Catholic Church, for example, a person can only be considered as having committed a sin if they are mentally competent. The psychiatric disorder may, therefore, mitigate the interpretation of voluntary death as a sin.

In Hinduism, the central belief in reincarnation and karma softens the condemnation of suicide, because death is not seen as the end of life but rather the beginning of one's rebirth. This religion's stance on self-inflicted death has been ambiguous. It reinforces the unacceptable nature of it, but on the other hand, Hinduism condones religious suicides. Generally speaking, it is discouraged within the Hindu faith.

For Muslims, suicide is expressly forbidden in the Holy Quran in Surah 4 in two verses:

Verse 29[10]: *O you who have believed, do not consume one another's wealth unjustly but only [in lawful] business by mutual consent. And do not kill yourselves [or one another]. Indeed, Allah is to you ever Merciful.*

Verse 30[11]: *And whoever does that in aggression and injustice - then We will drive him into a Fire. And that, for Allah, is [always] easy.*

Suicidal ideation is also rejected in Islam. Those who take their own lives are condemned to eternal repetitions of the act. Moreover, many Islamic countries have incorporated Sharia Islamic law as part of their legal systems, including Qatar, Singapore, Somalia, United Arab Emirates, Iraq, Afghanistan, Iran, and Saudi Arabia, which holds one of the strictest interpretations of such law. As mentioned at the beginning of this chapter, in some of these countries, suicide is considered a crime.

Although it is hard to make a direct impact between religious condemnation of self-inflicted death and actual attempts, religion is considered a protective factor against completed suicide. In one of the few long-term longitudinal studies conducted in the United States about this, researchers Evan Kleiman and Richard Liu found[12] that people who attended religious services twenty-four times or more per year were less than half as likely to die by suicide as those who did not.

Other cultural factors

In Japan, which holds the thirtieth position in WHO's global rates, it is believed that a culture of tolerance to suicide may be one of the factors encouraging such practice. Among historical examples are the Harakiri and Seppuku —a suicidal ritual in which the individual cut their stomach open with a sword—and the kamikaze, Japanese pilots who, during World War II, dove their planes toward enemy targets. Since 2005, this country has adopted a series of actions to combat self-inflicted death. Japan's Basic Act for Suicide Prevention was signed into law in June 2006, followed by specific additional policies in 2007. In 2012, the country's general principles were revised to focus on the youth and those who have attempted suicide[13].

India

India has received much attention worldwide due to its high rates and a particular gender-related aspect. The country is currently in the nineteenth position on WHO's rankings, with a rate of 16.5 per 100,000, responsible due to its large population for 37 percent of all the world's suicides of women and 26 percent of men's[14]. In 2016, a number of researchers examined India's data and came to some startling conclusions. They observed a 40-percent rise from 1990-2016, and although the country follows the global trend of more men dying from suicide than women, the difference is not as high as in the rest of the world: 21 per 100,000 for men and 15 for women.

When looking at both sexes combined, suicide is the leading cause of death for the 15-39 age group. In young women ages 15-29, self-inflicted death was the first cause of death in twenty-six of the country's thirty-one states. Some of the reasons behind the higher rates for younger women are directly related to gender roles and marriage. In India, early and arranged marriages are common, which lead to financial dependence and the responsibilities of motherhood in young females. Domestic violence and lack of access to mental health services have also played a part.

In India, female suicide is tolerated to some extent. From 316 BC to 1829 AD, when the British abolished such practice, it was expected that when their husbands passed, the women would set themselves on fire as a sign of respect. Such ritual is named *suttee, sati* in Sanskrit, which means "true wife." Even though the practice is not legally allowed anymore, this type of death can still be found in some corners of the country. An important measure has recently been taken, however. In 2017, India passed its Mental Healthcare Act[15], which determines that those who attempt suicide should not be penalized anymore due to the distress and possible mental illness associated with the act.

References

[1] https://www.who.int/gho/mental_health/suicide_rates/en/

[2] http://psychopathology.imedpub.com/suicides-in-russia-and-belarus-a-comparative-analysis-of-trends.php?aid=7536

[3] A map with world alcohol consumption can be seen here: https://ourworldindata.org/alcohol-consumption

[4] http://www.healthdata.org/research-article/global-regional-and-national-burden-suicide-mortality-1990-2016-systematic-analysis

[5] http://www.abs.gov.au/ausstats/abs@.nsf/Lookup/by%20

Subject/3303.0~2017~Main%20Features~Intentional%20self-harm,%20 key%20characteristics~3

[6] https://www.ons.gov.uk/peoplepopulationandcommunity/ birthsdeathsandmarriages/deaths/bulletins/ suicidesintheunitedkingdom/2017registrations

[7] Jamison, K. (2000). Night falls fast: understanding suicide. New York, NY: Random House.

[8] https://linguistics.ucla.edu/people/grads/connormayer/papers/ cmayer_note_to_an_old_friend.pdf

[9] https://www.myjewishlearning.com/article/suicide-in-jewish-tradition-and-literature/

[10] https://quran.com/4/29

[11] https://quran.com/4/30-40?translations=20

[12] Kleiman, E., & Liu, R. (2014). Prospective prediction of suicide in a nationally representative sample: Religious service attendance as a protective factor. British Journal of Psychiatry, 204(4), 262-266. doi:10.1192/bjp.bp.113.128900

[13] https://www.who.int/mental_health/suicide-prevention/en/

[14] https://www.thelancet.com/journals/lanpub/article/PIIS2468-2667(18)30138-5/fulltext

[15] https://indiacode.nic.in/handle/123456789/2249?view_ type=search&sam_handle=123456789/1362

CHAPTER FOUR

Risk Factors

When analyzed on the individual level, suicide can be the result of a combination of social, biological, psychological, and environmental aspects. Although multifaceted, experts agree that when present, some factors predispose an individual to voluntary death. Often, they intertwine, forming intricate paths that may result in self-destruction. Knowing such elements is an important step to prevention.

In order of importance, the main risk factors associated with suicide are previous attempts, family history of suicide, mental disorders (particularly clinical unipolar and bipolar depression), and abuse of psychoactive substances, such as alcohol and illicit drugs. Regarding mental illnesses, it should be noted that although they are closely related to self-inflicted death, the vast majority of people with such disorders never take their own lives. This is an important caveat, because it may help address and identify other issues related to the loss, as well as to destigmatize such illnesses.

Other factors are regularly correlated with suicide: feelings of hopelessness, aggressive and impulsive behavior, cultural and religious beliefs, isolation, barriers to accessing mental health treatment, physical illness, easy access to lethal methods, unwillingness to seek help due to stigma, and loss (death of a loved one, job loss, financial collapse, etc.).

Previous attempt

When a person has a history of attempting suicide, one must stay alert. According to the American Foundation for Suicide Prevention[1], in 2017, approximately 1,400,000 people attempted suicide in the United States. The data is made available by the Center for Disease Control (CDC) based on surveys and reports sent by hospitals on non-fatal injuries from self-harm. According to the 2017 National Survey of Drug Use and Mental Health, an estimated 0.6 percent of adults ages eighteen or older made at least one attempt. This translates to approximately 1.4 million adults. The financial costs are equally high, amounting to $69 billion for that year.

When it comes to age groups, the rates of attempted and completed suicide go in opposite directions. As a person grows older, self-inflicted death rates rise, while attempts decrease. Based on the 2017 Youth Risk Behaviors Survey, 7.4 percent of youth in grades nine to twelve reported that they had made at least one suicide attempt in the past twelve months, with female students doing it almost twice as often as male students (9.3 percent and 5.1 percent, respectively). In terms of race, the highest rates were found among black students, at 9.8 percent, with white students at 6.1 percent.

The age group with the highest percentage of suicidal thoughts in the United States is those between 18 and 25 years old.

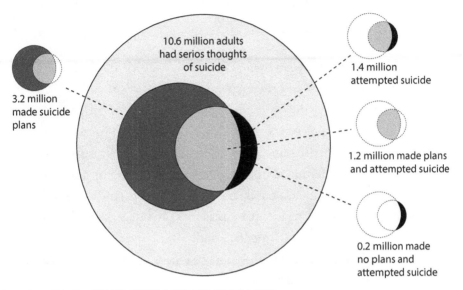

10.6 million adults had serios thoughts of suicide

3.2 million made suicide plans

1.4 million attempted suicide

1.2 million made plans and attempted suicide

0.2 million made no plans and attempted suicide

SOURCE: NATIONAL SURVEY ON DRUG USE AND HEALTH, 2017

Many times, those who attempt suicide present difficulties when dealing with stress, losses, and moments of crisis. For this reason, given the proper circumstances, they may try to take their own lives again. It is estimated that for every suicide death, there are around three hospitalizations and nine emergency room visits for attempt, and twenty-seven attempts that do not result in hospitalizations or emergency visits.

Mental disorders

It is important to note that although the association of suicide and mental disorders is well-established in high-income countries, the complex puzzle of self-inflicted death is composed of many other pieces, such as personal crisis (divorce, financial difficulties, abuse, violence, isolation, and various types of losses), low resilience to stress, and cultural components. Discrimination is another key aspect that contributes to the statistics. It affects specific marginalized groups, including the LGBTQ populations, migrants, refugees, prisoners, and indigenous peoples.

Historically, the link between mental health and suicide has been quite direct. Most institutions and researchers affirm that approximately 90 percent of people who die by voluntary death have an underlying mental illness. This percentage comes from the 1970s, when the founders of suicidology started performing psychological autopsies, a research tool used to collect information about an individual who died by suicide. By talking to the individual's family members, relatives, and friends, the researcher would try to identify stressors in the deceased's life, as well as possible symptoms of mental conditions, regardless of formal diagnosis. This percentage deserves a more current analysis and possible update, particularly when we look at data from countries with reliable surveillance systems, such as the United States.

The CDC found that in 2015, 54 percent of individuals who died by suicide did not have a known mental health condition, a percentage far higher than the 10 percent that is usually cited by specialists. This shift is very significant and calls our attention to consider other factors outside the medical realm, particularly when it comes to prevention programs, because historically, the focus of these initiatives has primarily prioritized mental health issues. As for additional factors, the CDC report[2] pointed to personal conflicts (such as relationship problems), criminal and legal matters, loss of/eviction from home, and other crises.

1. Depression

World Data (Source: World Health Organization (WHO, 2018))
- The disease affects 300 million people worldwide.

- It is the leading cause of disability worldwide.
- Fewer than half of those affected (in many countries, fewer than 10 percent) receive treatment.
- In most cases, the treatment combination of medication and psychotherapy is effective.

US Data (Source: National Institute of Mental Health, 2017)

- An estimated 17.3 million adults had at least one major depressive episode—approximately 7.1 percent of all U.S. adults.
- The prevalence was higher among adult females (8.7 percent) compared to males (5.3 percent) and highest among individuals ages 18-25 (13.1 percent).

Unipolar depression—the type that does not include mania—is the single psychiatric diagnosis most commonly associated with suicide. For this reason, the illness will be looked at in more detail than other risk factors. According to the American Association of Suicidology,[3] the risk of suicide among patients with untreated depression ranges from 2.2 percent to 15 percent. Approximately 15 percent of those who treat the disease eventually die by self-inflicted death. Between 5.2 and 9 percent of people who have been diagnosed with depression will complete suicide. Having the illness increases suicide risk twenty-five times when compared to the general population.

Before defining the main features of this disease, I would like to propose a reflection. The increasing pressure for quick happiness enforced in Western culture, greatly emphasized on social media, may play a dangerous role in the diagnosis of depression. When friends talk to me about 'being depressed,' I often try to listen to what is happening in their lives, because they might have strong reasons to be feeling sad or isolated, for example. It doesn't necessarily mean they need to see a doctor, however.

While trying to fit in and respond to external expectations of 'being ok,' 'getting over it,' and 'being strong,' internal issues (feelings and emotions) are relegated to the background. In many instances, when going through loss, we move away from what gives us emotional stability in the long run: solid personal relationships, strong values, connection, and purpose. We live in a culture of individualism, where the sense of community lies farther and farther away. What counts is personal success, which often means social status and appearances.

Throughout this trajectory, another imposition is constructed, that of avoiding suffering at any cost, and it is here that an error of evaluation is increasingly common: we confuse sadness with depression. There is little room for mourning when someone is gone, for crying because of a recent divorce, for expressing discontent and anger after being fired. We feel pressure to 'move on' without giving ourselves space to be human.

Instead of going through the natural process of grief, many times, pain is medicated based on the illusion that it will erase the source of suffering, to no avail. The Diagnostic and Statistical Manual of Mental Disorder (DSM-5), which is the main guide for diagnosing mental disorders in the USA, recognizes that it is necessary to differentiate a Major Depressive Episode (MDE) from the reactions experienced during bereavement.

Here are some noted differences:

- In grief, the predominant affect is feelings of emptiness and loss, while in an MDE it is a persistent, depressed mood and the inability to anticipate happiness or pleasure.
- The dysphoria in grief is likely to decrease in intensity over days to weeks, and it occurs in waves. The depressed mood is more persistent and is not tied to specific thoughts or preoccupations.

- The pain of grief may be accompanied by positive emotions and humor that are uncharacteristic of the pervasive unhappiness and misery characteristic of a major depressive episode.
- The thought content associated with grief generally features a preoccupation with thoughts and memories of the deceased, rather than the self-critical or pessimistic rumination seen in an MDE.
- In grief, self-esteem is generally preserved, whereas in an MDE, feelings of worthlessness and self-loathing are common.
- If a bereaved individual thinks about death and dying, such thoughts are generally focused on the deceased and possibly about "joining" the deceased, whereas in a major depressive episode, such thoughts are focused on ending one's own life because of feeling worthless, undeserving of life, or unable to cope with the pain of depression (p.126).

How do we know, then, that what we feel is no longer a mere sadness? Several aspects are taken into account—particularly, the duration of the symptoms, their intensity, and the way they are affecting the life of the individual. Among the main symptoms of depression, the following stand out:

- Loss of interest or pleasure in routine activities (anhedonia).
- Feeling sad for most of the day, almost every day.
- Isolation, blunted affect (difficulty responding to external stimuli).
- Carelessness with physical appearance.
- Hopelessness.
- Loss of libido.
- Weight loss or gain.

- Changes in sleep (too much sleep or waking up earlier than usual).

- Irritability, aggressiveness.

- Feeling of tiredness, weakness and lack of energy.

- Feeling worthless, guilty, a burden to others.

- Anxiety.

- Difficulty concentrating and making decisions, as well as memory difficulties.

- Frequent thoughts of death and suicide.

In general, symptoms should be present for a period of two weeks or more and should not be the cause of recent mourning. Depending on to what degree and in what ways it affects a person's life, the disease is classified as mild, moderate, or severe. It's important to ask: Is the individual able to function? Answering this question is key to diagnose depression.

Family mental health history has great relevance in depression. Having a family member with the illness by no means seals a person's fate, but it is certainly one more aspect that must be taken into consideration, just like in other types of diseases. The difference is that, with the stigma that accompanies mental illnesses, many ignore family history in an attempt to deny that they may be sick.

This happened with Fernanda, a thirty-three-year-old nurse I interviewed. She admitted her reluctance to face her depression even though the illness was present in some of her relatives:

"After all I've been through, I see today that there is a very large predisposition on the part of my mother's family. Two of her aunts had mental disorders. One chose suicide, not suicide in a conventional way, but a process perhaps even more painful for the family.

She hated taking a bath. When having to take one, three women were necessary to hold her; she would scream and say that they were killing her. And so it went on for a long time. She did not eat, and when she did, she vomited, and refused to take the antidepressants until the point that her body could not stand it, and she began languishing and died.

Years later, I started the treatment, but I stopped the drugs because I thought I did not need them. When the depression came back, it came stronger— that was when I started to plan suicide again. I was determined to kill myself.

I thought I had wasted my teenage years fighting cancer, and then I had a serious accident in which I lost my boyfriend and a great friend; they were years of suffering. I did not believe in anything anymore. I thought that love was very stupid, and I realize that in those times I did not have friends—people cannot stand to be around a depressive person.

My beliefs were fading away, I fell into a huge crisis. I cried for a week but managed to hide from everyone my suicide plans. I was preparing things; I wanted to do everything well away from my parents. I had already thought about it in detail. It would happen in a place far from home, without documents so as to leave no clues. I would make everything seem an accident, so my parents would not think it was suicide.

The only thing missing was money. I would need to save the money to go to this place. But one day, a friend called me, and I burst into tears. She recommended a doctor to me, but I didn't have any money, so she paid for the appointment. I saw a psychiatrist the following week—I decided to give myself that last chance. That friend insisted that I go, something that only a mother does for her daughter.

When I got to the psychiatrist's office and he saw the state I was in, he didn't even talk much; he just got a medication, gave it to me, and scheduled to see me again in a week. He explained to me that my problem was chemical, which we were going to treat with the drug.

For the first few days, I slept non-stop, but I had a wonderful feeling of well-being. During my second appointment, I was already better, and the first question he asked me was about suicide. I said I was not thinking about that anymore.

Today, I take medication, I'm feeling very well, and I know now that it's no use running away or trying to be Wonder Woman. You have to take it seriously and treat the disease. Psychiatry is here to help.

I want to forget what I've been through, but I need to let others hear my story so that I can give my contribution to those who have already been or are going through it. There are wonderful professionals who are magically placed in your life. A person who reaches the point of thinking about suicide believes he has nothing else to live for, but a single detail can save a life, change a story, and mine has been changed. I have depression, I am aware of it, and today I accept the illness.

The main thing I worried about was that I would spend my whole life dependent on a medication. Now, I see it differently. If I need to take it, I'll take it. I'm more aware. There's no point in running away from it. There may be a point when I won't need the drug anymore, but I'll always be on the alert for the symptoms."

Treatment

Social acceptance of depression has advanced considerably in recent years. Today, people are more comfortable talking about it, asking questions and understanding that this disease can be treated. Prejudice still exists, though, and this is one of the main factors that keep those affected by depression away from medical and counseling offices (in addition to the high cost and prolonged treatment time).

After the initial diagnosis, which should be done through careful evaluation, the doctor selects the appropriate antidepressant to be prescribed, but unlike other diseases, taking the medication doesn't mean instant relief, and that is a major barrier to effective treatment. When we have a headache, for example, a pill will likely bring the intensity of the pain down within a few minutes or hours. This does not happen with psychotropic medication. In most cases, they usually take an average of two weeks to start having noticeable effects. A lot of people give up on the treatment before that, or worse, stop as soon as they notice signs of improvement, a common mistake that can have serious consequences.

After the remission of symptoms, the medication should continue to be administered daily for at least six months. Depending on the severity of the case, medication can continue throughout one's lifetime. The effectiveness of the treatment depends greatly on the patient's discipline and their awareness of the disease's prognosis.

There are other factors that hinder the healing process. Even when the medication is effective, it is necessary to find the right dosage, which can sometimes take a few months, and not everybody responds to antidepressants at all. Another important note is that, when it comes to suicide, as much as this may sound like a contradiction, one of the risks associated with self-inflicted death is precisely the improvement of the depressive symptoms.

The explanation is actually quite simple. Many view depression as the opposite of joy but, in truth, the illness leads to a gradual state of apathy, the total absence of sensations and lack of will to act. When a patient starts to emerge from this lethargic state, there may be an intensification of suicidal thinking, and as they regain some of their energy, they feel ready to act and plan their own death. For this reason, when there is risk of suicide, at the beginning of treatment, psychiatrists usually frequently monitor patients' reactions to medication. With time, appointments become less frequent.

The journalist Andrew Solomon, who wrote *Noonday Demon: An Atlas of Depression* says: "The opposite of depression is vitality." He went through many of the stages of the disease, ultimately arriving at a point of paralysis. He also made the poor choice of stopping the medication, and suffered serious consequences as a result. During our conversation, he recalled how difficult it was to accept that he was depressed, something that, according to Andrew, took an unnecessary toll on his life:

"I had already had depression well before identifying the disease, because at the time I had no idea what it was. I was seeing an analyst who today I call 'the incompetent,' who insisted on saying: 'You are going through a difficult time and it is very brave of you to stand alone without medication.' Meanwhile, I only got worse to the point where I got so physically unbalanced that I could hardly move.

It used to take a full day to shower. Once, I remember feeling incredible terror, lying on the floor of the apartment, until I thought, 'This is out of control and destroying my life.' I knew there was something wrong, but like many people, I did not want to admit it, I thought I was strong and that I could solve the problem on my own. This attitude made the disease escalate. If I had started the treatment six months earlier, much suffering would have been avoided.

Today, I identify my first episode of depression as occurring in 1994, when I published a novel. The reviews were positive, but I did not care. I remember thinking, 'How strange, I always wanted to write a novel, I should be very happy with the reception, but I don't feel anything.' This was the beginning of dissociation.

Then everything became a burden. I would come home, and there were eight messages of congratulations on the answering machine. But all I could think about was the work I would have to do to return the calls. Anything required a great effort; every day it was as if another piece of my life was being included in this burden, until I was exhausted. 'My God, I have to eat, take the food from the refrigerator, put it on the plate, cut it, chew it and then swallow it,' I would say.

It was ridiculous. I didn't understand why I was having these problems, I was very hard on myself, but it was out of my control. Everything was very, very difficult.

When the anxiety came, it became intolerable. I felt overwhelmed all the time, as if I'd just jumped from a plane and was close to hitting the ground. From then on, I was unable to carry out my daily activities, such as getting out of bed, bathing, eating, sleeping.

I was paralyzed in a state of frantic despair, so I thought, 'I can't go on like this.' It was at this point that I began to think suicidal thoughts. It wasn't that I was afraid of the rest of my life—what I couldn't stand was the idea of living the next five minutes feeling that way. It was so painful to be alive. It was at that time that I began to crumble.

On October 30 of the same year, on my birthday, I had dinner scheduled at a restaurant with my father, brother, sister-in-law, and a few friends. It was a light, intimate group, but I realized that I could not get dressed, couldn't leave the apartment, couldn't do anything. I called my father saying I was feeling terrible, so he asked if I wanted them to bring me the cake, and I said 'okay.'

When they arrived, I was afraid to get out of bed and interact with them. My father asked what was happening, said that I seemed to be in a terrible state and asked if I was well. I said, 'No, I'm not, I need help.' I had lost a lot of weight and couldn't even eat the cake.

I've had other episodes, but that one was the worst, because I'd never been through that. Today, when I start to feel bad, it is bad, but at least rationally I know that I have been through it and that I will improve. The first time is different, because the feeling is that you will feel that way forever.

The next day, I went to see a psychopharmacologist. The medication has been extremely important to me. It pulled me out of the intense depression. I don't believe that I would have left the crises without the drug, and I continue to take it—it is crucial for me. I stopped several times, but I was fine for a short time and then I felt bad again, so I decided that I would not allow myself to go through that suffering anymore.

Even with all this, I had to get accustomed to the image that I am a person who takes antidepressants, who has an illness and is in treatment.

It took a long time to integrate into my sense of reality the idea that I would no longer be able to be myself without this kind of intervention. But I have a disease that is real."

Identifying the psychological causes

It is widely accepted that the association between medication and psychotherapy is the most efficient way to deal with depression. In many cases, the disease comes as a consequence of internal difficulties in dealing with pain, stress, loss and daily struggles. In 2014, researchers conducted a meta-analysis[4] of fifty-two articles that compared the results of combined pharmacotherapy and psychotherapy in adults with depression and anxiety disorders.

The sample included 3,623 patients from the United States and Europe—1,767 were treated with medication and therapy and 1,856 only with drugs. The researchers concluded that the combined approach was more effective for major depression, panic disorder and Obsessive Compulsive Disorder up to two years after treatment. In their view, therapy with only psychotropic medication is not the best option for common mental disorders.

Although suicide prevention is well-advanced in the United States, where the subject is treated as a public health issue, even in that country there is a tendency to deal with a suicidal person as a patient who needs diagnosis and medication. Dr. Edwin Shneidman, responsible for opening the first suicide prevention center in the United States in 1958, argues the opposite:

"Suicide is identified as a type of depression, which intellectually comes from nineteenth-century psychiatry. The Diagnostic and Statistical Manual, DSM-IV⁵, treats it as if it were a liver or a kidney. I believe there is a huge amount of psychological pain in the world without suicide, but there is no suicide without enormous psychological pain.

The name of this pain is psychic pain—that is, located in the mind of the individual. It is the pain of negative emotion as shame and loneliness. The suicide is a state of acute disruption. The person is unhappy about the status quo and wants to modify it, so the act is an effort to stop the flow of pain.

My clinical approach isn't to establish a psychiatric diagnosis, nor even to know the family history. Both are important, but they are not central. The focus is to answer two questions: 'Where does it hurt?' and 'How can I help you?' The way to prevent suicide is to identify the source of the pain, then address it correctly. Suicide is not a brain disease, it is a disturbance of the mind, a psychological storm."

Another limitation of a treatment that is strictly based on medication is that, although it helps regulate brain chemistry, it does not contribute to the psychological aspects that underlie depression. This is why the ideal path is to combine drugs with therapy.

A recurring criticism of those who advocate the combined approach is the fact that there are still a large number of physicians who place all the expectation of cure on antidepressants alone. Antônio Carlos Garcia worked as a psychiatrist for fifteen years, then enrolled in the first group of the Brazilian Society of Analytical Psychology, today his area of activity. He criticizes the excess of prescription drugs:

"What I feel in my fellow psychiatrists is that they are more organic than

any doctor—strangely, paradoxically, because of their academic training they should not be. I think the psychiatrist has a certain complex of inhabiting a half-border area between organic medicine and psychology, so he wants, through this complex, to identify himself in organic things. Psychiatry in recent years has been very organic, because I also think that there are very strong, very powerful economic factors, those that force psychiatry to go biologically to certain lines.

What we see in psychiatry is exactly that it is a very ideological science and even subjected to intense economic forces. If I'm not mistaken, the global budget for psychotropics in the pharmaceutical industry is greater than that of the war industry, so you imagine that the pharmaceutical industry forces a great ideological load within the clinical researches that are done in psychiatry.

Psychiatrists nowadays—of course I'm not talking about all my colleagues—believe that psychotropic medication comes as close to happiness as possible and that drugs will resolve great human problems. As a psychiatrist, I do not think that drugs solve major human problems. I think it's a therapeutic arsenal for treating certain diseases—a support, nothing more.

Personal reflection is definitely out of fashion; people want practical, immediate solutions. Drugs promise that. Without having to think about your problems, there is no need to examine what you are doing in your life. You only have to take them.

They are easy and tempting promises, so in that sense, I will not blame psychiatrists alone. It's a cultural issue. We are living in a time of instant gratification."

Garcia cites the example of a patient who came to his office with suicidal ideation. Through psychodrama, he asked her to perform her own death using the method of choice:

"I said: So let's do this, let's carry out your suicide. She revealed that she

wanted to throw herself from a window. I said, 'Good, would you like to dramatize what this suicide would look like?'

I had her come up on my desk, showed her where the window would be, and told her to jump, fall on the floor, close her eyes, and imagine herself dead, and she did exactly that. I asked her to remain dead, to imagine how things would be like. At the funeral, she saw her mother, her brothers, her friends arriving, and she felt great pleasure in seeing her mother and siblings cry and suffer over her death. She had finally managed to make them acknowledge her existence. The patient realized that what she really wanted was to hurt them.

This is an individual case, of course. We cannot generalize it or conclude that all suicidal people want to do this. I'm just showing how I work as a psychoanalyst. I'm going to guide my client to find out what their symbolic representations stand for, and of course that is absolutely unique. It will be different for each person.

Death is a symbol of transformation, the greatest symbol of all, and every symbol sprouts from the unconscious. Suicide is a great mistake. What the person wants is to kill things on the inside, to transform their life, but they think themselves incapable of doing this and cannot see because we tend to think rationally, so it blocks us from seeing the symbols."

Many times, in the search for symbolic meanings, the patient confronts themself with the unknown, with associations and feelings that, until then, were not part of their own conception of "self". When they come into contact with pain, they must learn to identify what the true meanings of the pain are. This is when the therapist comes in. The therapist's role is to carefully lead the patient through this path with empathy and compassion.

The Brazilian psychoanalyst Evaldo Melo makes a helpful distinction between the optics of the psychoanalyst and of those who see medication as the only means of cure:

"Depression as a disease (which is quite different from depressive traits) is a complex condition characterized by various symptoms. Speaking as a psychoanalyst, disease is always a consequence, not the cause. But those who follow the medical model will say that it is a hereditary pathology and it is this hereditary element that causes the illness. I think that all mental illnesses, be it depression, anxiety or schizophrenia, are always an adaptive response of the mind to pain, to suffering, to some kind of suffering, to a deprivation."

2. Bipolar disorder

Although depression is at the top of the list when it comes to suicide risk, other conditions require attention. According to the Diagnostic and Statistical Manual for Mental Disorders, DSM-5, the lifetime risk of suicide in individuals with bipolar disorder is estimated to be at least fifteen times that of the general population.

In her acclaimed book A Restless Mind, the Johns Hopkins School of Medicine's psychiatrist professor, Kay Jamison, speaks of living with bipolarity[6]:

"There is a particular kind of pain, elation, loneliness, and terror involved in this kind of madness. When you're high it's tremendous. The ideas and feelings are fast and frequent like shooting stars, and you follow them until you find better and brighter ones.

Shyness goes, the right words and gestures are suddenly there, the power to captivate others a felt certainty. There are interests found in uninteresting people. Sensuality is pervasive and the desire to seduce and be seduced irresistible. Feelings of ease, intensity, power, well-being, financial omnipotence, and euphoria pervade one's marrow. But, somewhere, this changes.

The fast ideas are far too fast, and there are far too many; overwhelming confusion replaces clarity. Memory goes. Humour and absorption on friends' faces are replaced by fear and concern. Everything previously moving with the grain is now against—you are irritable, angry, frightened, uncontrollable, and enmeshed totally in the blackest caves of the mind. You never knew those caves were there.

It will never end, for madness carves its own reality.

... Manic-depression distorts moods and thoughts, incites dreadful behaviors, destroys the basis of rational thought, and too often erodes the desire and will to live. It is an illness that is biological in its origins, yet one that feels psychological in the experience of it, an illness that is unique in conferring advantage and pleasure, yet one that brings in its wake almost unendurable suffering and, not infrequently, suicide."

Treatment

Even in the most severe forms, Bipolar Disorder can be stabilized with the use of medication. Usually, the treatment is lifelong with a combination of drugs, mainly mood stabilizers, antipsychotics, and antidepressants. The same caveats should be made regarding the need to take a multidisciplinary approach to treatment. Psychotropic medication is not a one-size-fits-all solution.

In the beginning of her treatment, Kay Jamison remembers that she went into "a war" with the medication. She stopped several times, provoking increasingly intense episodes. After her illness was stabilized, she created a kind of manual. With wit and humor, she guides those who need to get accustomed to the effects of lithium:

- *Clear out the medicine cabinet before guests arrive for dinner or new lovers stay the night.*

- *Remember to put the lithium back into the cabinet the next day.*

- *Don't be too embarrassed by your lack of coordination or your inability to do well the sports you once did with ease.*

- *Learn to laugh about spilling coffee, having the palsied signature of an eighty-year-old, and being unable to put on cufflinks in less than ten minutes.*

- *Smile when people joke about how they think they "need to be on lithium."*

- *Nod intelligently, and with conviction, when your physician explains to you the many advantages of lithium in leveling out the chaos in your life.*

- *Be patient when waiting for this leveling off. Very patient. Reread the Book of Job. Continue being patient. Contemplate the similarity between the phrases "being patient" and "being a patient."*

- *Try not to let the fact that you can't read without effort annoy you. Be philosophical. Even if you could read, you probably wouldn't remember most of it anyway.*

- *Accommodate to a certain lack of enthusiasm and bounce that you once had. Try not to think about all the wild nights you once had. Probably best not to have had those nights anyway.*

- *Always keep in perspective how much better you are. Everyone else certainly points it out often enough, and, annoyingly enough, it's probably true.*

- *Be appreciative. Don't even consider stopping your lithium.*

- *When you do stop, get manic, get depressed, expect to hear two basic themes from your family, friends, and healers:*

  - *"But you were doing so much better, I just don't understand it."*

  - *"I told you this would happen."*

- *Restock your medicine cabinet.*

3. Alcohol and substance abuse

The way each person deals with pain leads them down different paths—one of those is the attempt to escape the suffering by numbing the pain. This is one of the major roles of drugs, including alcohol. They serve as self-medication. There are several risks associated with the use of these substances, including addiction—which can lead to increased aggression and physical and psychological damage—and death, voluntary or not.

Most prevention strategies include decreasing access to alcohol as a suggested measure. In 2015, researchers reviewed seventeen articles that analyzed the impact of restrictive policies on suicide rates in the United States and internationally[7]. The results showed a positive effect on reducing self-inflicted death, as well as decreased levels of alcohol involvement among suicide decedents.

It is important to note that in many cases, it is difficult to separate the correlation between risk factors, since one may lead to another. Depression and alcohol are a good example. Patients commonly drink to relieve symptoms, but the opposite also occurs. Substance abuse leads to social disintegration (divorce, loss of family bonds, unemployment). As a result, the individual isolates themself and can, from this isolation, develop symptoms of depression, therefore boosting the risk of suicide.

Another factor directly associated with alcohol is the loss of self-esteem, which also raises the risk of developing depression. Alcohol causes many behavioral changes. It increases impulsivity and aggressive tendencies while reducing restrictions on dangerous behaviors. All these elements are directly related to suicide.

When I interviewed Fernanda, a nurse in her early thirties, she told me that after her first episode of depression, she self-medicated with alcohol. Suicidal ideation came next.

"*I decided to take my life. Only I could make that decision, after all—the life was mine, the pain was mine, nobody could do anything for me. But I thought I had to tell my parents to let them know it was my decision. I did not want to punish them, but to prepare them.*

I called my mother for a serious conversation and said, 'Look, Mom, I can't take the burden that is my life, the pain, so I have decided to die. I'll do it in a way that no one will suffer, me neither, I just wish you would forgive me and accept my decision.'

I cannot imagine the pain she felt, I just heard her scream a cry of anguish. That broke me up. At that moment, with all his humility and wisdom, my father talked to me, and said: 'Daughter, can't you wait a few days? Because I don't have the financial means to make a decent burial for you, I am in a lot of debt.'

At that time, the expression of his eyes filled with tears registered in my brain. I saw the eyes of a simple, hard-working, honest man suffering because of me. The truth is that I was living in a terrible darkness—the sun would shine, but all I could see was darkness. It came from my soul. I did not want to see anyone else suffer for me, especially my parents.

I couldn't stand that torture anymore, I was full of debts that my boyfriend had left in my name, seeing my father working to help me. I was determined to take my life. The moment my father left my house, I closed the door and said, 'It's now.'

I made a mix of various medications, antidepressants, strong analgesics, etc. I put the rubber on my arm, I took the vein, but I did not have the strength to inject. I believe it was due to the suffering of my parents, because I saw that they still needed me. I could not leave them alone at that moment.

Anyway, I had to do something to ease the pain, so I started to drink. I was taking antidepressants and drinking a bottle of wine a day. What did I do? I would turn on the radio, open a bottle of wine, drink, drink, and take another antidepressant.

No one noticed because I only drank at night, when everyone was asleep.

The drinking made me stay happy, light, so people thought I was recovering—even I believed that. The only person who noticed that I was drinking too much was my brother, and even then he did not say anything, he just asked me to control it. He could not imagine the gravity of the situation.

The medication obviously had no effect. The psychiatrist who treated me did not charge for the appointments, which made me rush them so I would not take a lot of his time. I would sit and say that I was not well, and that was it. I wouldn't even mention the drinking. She would change the medication, and send me off. With time, things began to improve. I started to have hope, then I thought: I'm going to get this idea of suicide out of my head."

In her case, alcohol was a means to avoid pain. The same happened to the Iranian Mahnaz, only for her, the drug of choice was Valium, an anxiolytic and sedative used in the treatment of anxiety. After the troubled and violent divorce of her parents and the abrupt entry of a new family into her life she was sent to India with her two brothers. She had just attempted suicide for the second time, at age fourteen. Depressed and with no support, Mahnaz dived into a life of self-destructive rituals:

"My father was very angry with me and said that he hoped that I would die, because I was destroying the reputation of the family. I stayed away from my mother, my friends, my country. I begged him to take me back. It was two years of crying every day, but nothing worked.

At that time, I met a girl who was dating my brother, and she had cut his name on her wrist. I thought, 'I could do that.' The psychological pain was so big, it worked as an escape, at least I was doing something. This became a daily habit, and over the time I would increase the depth of the cuts, always in the same place.

My brothers noticed, but they did not talk about it, because to them I was a burden, because they wanted to go out all the time and they had to come back home to stay with me. We rarely spoke to each other. My mother also knew but had other problems to take care of—I was not a priority.

Then I found another way out. I started taking a Valium a day. With time, I increased the dose. Two, three, four pills, until I took it non-stop. I was never awake. Sleeping was the only way I found to endure life. That lasted about six months. One day, I woke up and left the house, and people looked at me and said, 'You look great, how did you lose so much weight?'"

Understanding the numbing effect of substance use does not mean we should be complacent with it, says psychiatrist Dr. Sérgio Baldassin:

"We can even understand that the drug sometimes works as an anesthetic for pain or to fill a void, but we cannot endorse it. What this individual is saying is that the drug is his medicine and there is no other way out. We should ask if this is the only way, if there are no alternatives to not kill himself, to feel better. Sometimes he sees no way out, and thinks that's the only thing to do."

Other risk factors

- Serious physical health conditions.
- Access to lethal means (firearms and drugs).
- Prolonged stress.
- Stressful life events (rejection, divorce, loss, financial crisis).
- Exposure to another person's suicide.
- Childhood abuse, neglect, or trauma.
- Social isolation.
- Chronic pain.

Protective factors

- Access to mental health treatment.
- Strong connections to individuals, family, community, and social institutions.
- Personal traits such as optimism, impulse control, resilience, and ability to cope with and adapt to change.
- Self-esteem and a sense of purpose or meaning in life.
- Cultural, religious, or personal beliefs that discourage suicide.

References

[1] https://afsp.org/about-suicide/suicide-statistics/

[2] https://www.cdc.gov/mmwr/volumes/67/wr/mm6722a1.htm?s_cid=mm6722a1_w#T1_down

[3] https://www.suicidology.org/portals/14/docs/resources/factsheets/2011/depressionsuicide2014.pdf

[4] Cuijpers, P., Sijbrandij, M., Koole, S. L., Andersson, G., Beekman, A. T., & Reynolds, C. F. (2014). Adding psychotherapy to antidepressant medication in depression and anxiety disorders: a meta-analysis. World Psychiatry, 13(1), 56–67. https://doi.org/10.1002/wps.20089

[5] The DSM was updated to its 5th version since I interviewed him, but with not much change in the way it sees depression.

[6] Jamison, K. (1999). Night Falls Fast: understanding suicide. United States, Vintage Books.

[7] Alcohol Policies and Suicide: A Review of the Literature - Xuan - 2016 - Alcoholism: Clinical and Exper-imental Research - Wiley Online Library. (n.d.). Retrieved April 5, 2019, from https://onlinelibrary-wiley-com.georgefox.idm.oclc.org/doi/full/10.1111/acer.13203

CHAPTER FIVE

Warning Signs

The day before my father killed himself, my older sister Renata noticed that he had stopped making future plans, even short-term ones. He came to visit her on a Sunday, and I would arrive from abroad the following Thursday. Dad would always pick us up at the airport, but when Renata asked him about it, he went on a tangent and talked about a trip he and I had taken a few years prior. This unusual behavior left her with an eerie feeling that something was wrong.

What Renata experienced is more common than you might think. The vast majority of people who complete suicide give warning signs before killing themselves. These verbal and nonverbal clues can be calls for help, and they originate in the ambiguity present in suicidal ideation. The person simultaneously hopes to end the pain and be rescued back to a life worth living. For those around them, the difficulty lies in identifying these signs and knowing what to do in case they suspect that there are risks of self-harm.

Expressing the pain

In general, such signs—whether verbal or non-verbal—indicate that the person does not plan to be around in the near future. Sentences like "I can't take it anymore," "I want to die," "You'd be better off without me," and "I'd like to disappear from this world" should never be ignored.

But there are also unsaid words that linger and can be conveyed by facial expression, body language, and even silence. That's what happened to my father. At no point did he tell Renata that he wasn't going to pick me up or that he would not be alive anymore by the following Thursday. He just refused to make plans. This is a good example of silence as an indication of farewell.

The psychoanalyst Edwin Shneidman, one of the foremost experts on the subject, singles out the word 'only' as the most dangerous in the study of suicide, because it expresses one of the strongest characteristics of the person planning to die: psychological and cognitive constriction, or what he calls 'Presuicidal Syndrome.' This is related to the individual's inability to see any option other than death as a way out. In English, the term is tunneling of vision, as if the person were in a tunnel and had lost the ability to look to the sides. Their focus blocks them from seeing additional perspectives.

This is what happened to Marisa, one of the people interviewed for this book. At the age of twenty-nine, she tried to kill herself, soon after having her second child. Her marriage was not going well, and the pregnancy was unwanted. When the baby boy was born, she rejected him, probably the result of postpartum depression. Marisa didn't have open communication with her parents—her upbringing was quite rigid. She also had a distant relationship with her brother. Her perception was that she only had one option:

"My marriage was in a crisis, and I got pregnant. I lost my mind. All I thought was that I would bring another child into this world to suffer. It was not fair. I had depression the whole pregnancy, and when he was born, I rejected him. I refused to take him home and instead left him at my mother's. It would be two or three days before I saw the baby again, and for me it didn't make a difference.

My husband kept trying to understand what was happening, and then he started to give me support. He saw that it was not something I was doing willingly. One day, we arrived at my mother's house, and I was so out of control that he had to break into the laundry room where I was trying to kill myself with a knife pointed at my stomach. If he hadn't arrived in that moment, I don't even know what would have happened.

I thought it was the only solution. I couldn't stand it any longer—I had an emptiness inside of me. I said to him: 'I'm no good, I don't know why I'm here. I'm going to give everyone relief, including myself. I've had enough. What will I stay here for? If I die, it's over, and life goes on. People will suffer a little, but it will pass.' As for my children, I believed it was better than having a crazy mother.

One day, my daughter said to her grandfather, 'It's good my father installed bars on the apartment windows, or my mother would have jumped today.' She was only two years old. I fell apart; I didn't have the right to do that. My two-year-old daughter was seeing this. What example was I giving her? I didn't want her to see me as a weak person, so I decided to seek therapy.

I spent four years in treatment, and for twelve months, all I did was cry. Today, I see what was happening. The problem was not my marriage; the problem came from way back. The marriage only aggravated the depression. It was an accumulation of everything. I had stopped working, and I would think, 'Wow, I studied so hard just to stay home taking care of kids.' It wasn't what I wanted.

I had to make up for lost time with my son. Today, I see that all the symptoms he had from being rejected are gone, because I have been able to rebuild our relationship."

The feeling of hopelessness is one of the most verbalized feelings in suicidal ideation. "I can't go on like this," "this life does not make sense," "it's hopeless," and "nothing matters" are common sentences.

Behavioral cues

Suicidal people experience symptoms and develop behaviors that are similar to those found in clinical depression: sleep impairment, substance abuse, seclusion, tiredness, loss of interest in formerly pleasurable activities, physical pain, isolation, disregard for appearance, mood changes, weight gain/loss, and apathy.

Other signs are also commonly characteristic of suicide and may indicate that the ideation has advanced to a more detailed plan. The individual who is planning their death may attend to practical things. They may write a will and distribute personal objects, including those that have a sentimental value. On the list of practical measures comes the organization of finances. Before he died, my father consolidated his bank accounts, paid all outstanding debts, and wrote me a letter in which he pointed out everything he would like me to do with his material things and assets. The document was posted two days before he died, and I received it one day after his death.

Some will also develop a particular interest in poems and other texts that deal with suicide and death, adopt careless behavior, and engage in dangerous situations. It is as if they are testing life, always putting themselves at risk. Andrew Solomon, author of *The Noonday Demon: An Atlas of Depression*, participated, along with his brother and father, in his mother's suicide. She had been battling cancer for years and had warned the family that if she reached a level of unbearable suffering, she would take her own life. Everyone conceded.

On the day she decided to die, the family gathered in her room for farewells. After the funeral, Andrew took with him the rest of the medication they had purchased for the suicide. Deep down, he wanted to make sure that if the same thing happened to him, he could take the rest. In the book, he writes that although he agreed with his mother's choice, the loss was internally overwhelming for him, and with time, he became increasingly consumed by guilt.

During an episode of depression, Andrew chose a drastic exit to the pain, as he portrays in his book:

"I could not figure out how to give myself cancer or MS or various other fatal diseases, but I knew just how to get AIDS, so I decided to do that. In a park in London, at a lonely hour well after midnight, a short, tubby man with thick tortoiseshell glasses came up and offered himself to me. He pulled down his trousers and bent over.

I went to work. I felt as though this were all happening to someone else; I heard his glasses fall off and thought only this: soon I will be dead, so I will never become old and sad like this man. A voice in my head said I had finally started this process and would soon die. I felt such a sense of release and of gratitude. It was not my intention to die slowly of AIDS; it was my intention to kill myself with HIV as my excuse."

Andrew recovered from depression and had a negative HIV test. During an interview, he explained to me the way he now interprets what he did at that time:

"I had always been very attached to my mother, and I believe that I was not prepared psychologically for the reality of an intense loss. I really believed in her decision, that it was right for my mother and for all of us. She wanted a death with dignity, and that's what she got, but I think that to see a scene of your mother swallowing pills to die was just too much. You see her asleep and think, 'If only I

could wake her up.'

But I watched and let it happen; it was agonizing. Today, I think of that moment with a lot of guilt, sadness, and anger. All this combined with the emotional loss brought on by her death, someone who was so close to me. There are layers upon layers of sadness.

I kept what was left of the medication she took. I thought that perhaps one day I would want to do the same. I over-identified myself with the loss of my mother. I thought, 'If she did this, should I also kill myself if the depression becomes a terminal condition?' In my mind, that opened up a range of possibilities.

As for AIDS, I may not have really tried to get the disease. I see that it had a lot to do with the thoughts associated with my mother's death, that the only way to kill myself would be by contracting a lethal disease. That it would give me a type of permission. At the time, this line of thought made all the sense in the world.

During the depression I made such an effort to stay alive that I dreamed of not having to wake up, get up, eat, work, sleep. It was all so tiring, so I wanted to find an acceptable way of not having to do any of it."

Among the most common warning signs of suicide, one of them stands out for its deceptive characteristics. It is marked by an apparent tranquility and emotional improvement in the person, which is usually far from their internal reality. The person, who might have been depressed or anxious, for example, seems to be better, in higher spirits, more focused, or generally out of crisis mode. This sends a misleading message to their family and friends. What actually happens is that, contrary to what is being perceived by others, the decision to die has been solidified; there is no more conflict or doubt, so the person becomes calmer, and seems from the outside to have improved.

In cases like this, it is frequent to hear, "But he seemed to be doing so well; he was upbeat, more optimistic, recovering." There is a sense of serenity, which is not necessarily untrue, but it's not occurring for the reason others believe. By eliminating the internal conflict, the person feels at peace, because they know that soon the pain will cease to exist.

After making the decision, the individual carries out the practical arrangements by visiting old friends, not worrying about previous sources of distress, going to places that take them back to their childhood, and organizing what will be left behind. Tom Hunt writes about this state of mind in *Cliffs of Despair: A Journey to the Edge:*

> *"But if you know your pain is about to end, wouldn't it be normal to be calm?"*[1]

Later on, close friends and family member look back and feel remorseful, because they didn't notice that such a turnaround was just a natural reaction of someone who had no more concerns about their future, due to the simple fact that in their minds, there was no more future to worry about.

What to do

This is a central question when it comes to suicidal ideation. What should we do when we notice that someone is thinking about killing themselves? The first suggestion sounds simple, but it is not as easy to carry out: speak directly about their ideation. Ask, very carefully, if the thought exists, and if so at what level, and the extent of their plan. You should never judge their attitude or mental state; there is no right or wrong, there is only an unbearable pain that they can't live with anymore.

Moral questioning has no relevance when it comes to suicide; it only makes matter worse, because it will provoke even stronger feelings of isolation and inadequacy in those who are already vulnerable to self-inflicted death.

The following are examples of direct, non-judgmental options:

- Have you ever thought about taking your life?
- Are you thinking about it now?
- Have you ever planned suicide? How far did you go with your plans?
- Do you think life is not worth living?
- Can you identify any other options for your current situation?

These questions allow us to carefully dig deeper into the issue, giving the other person the opportunity to express the sources of their despair. The American Association of Suicidology adds that, at the end of the conversation, we should try to establish a pact in which the suicidal person promises to contact us if the ideation reoccurs. In case of planning, it is imperative that you draw up a safety plan that includes other people. Family members, friends, institutions, and support organizations are some of the potential options.

Another frequent reaction that should be avoided is to display shock, because it will likely distance you further from the person. It is important to not only demonstrate calm, but also willingness to listen and openness to understanding their distress. No matter how futile or exaggerated it may seem to you, keep in mind that for the person in front of you, their problem is insurmountable and has become the center of their life.

Here is another example to be avoided: "But you have a healthy family, a good financial situation," or "You have everything." This kind of discussion is not helpful. Usually, rational thinking is beside the point and will make no difference whatsoever. We are dealing with emotions, not reasoning. They know they have a family, they know they have more than most people, but their psychological and emotional pain surpasses any logic. The value of life does not mean the same thing to them as it does to you; the weight of it all is totally out of balance.

Show that you are available. Sometimes, this attitude is enough to dampen their feeling of isolation. It is important that they know there is someone they can turn to in a moment of crisis. This happened with me. One day, I received a telephone call from a friend. At the time, I was already highly aware of warning signs, to the degree that by the tone of her voice, I could identify that she was calling to say goodbye.

I asked in a straightforward manner, "Are you thinking about killing yourself?" She started to cry and went on to say that everything was planned for the following week. She was taking a bus to a rural area of the state, far from her parents' home, where she would end her life. I asked her to give me some time, urged her to see a psychiatrist, and took her to see him the following Monday. She is still alive today.

One final note: however distorted it may seem, it is the reality of the person's life that matters. Never doubt the person's capacity to carry out a suicide attempt by saying things like, "You wouldn't do that." This attitude may serve as a trigger for the person to show that they are being serious.

Additional warning signs:

- Hopelessness.
- Uncontrolled hatred or anger, sometimes accompanied by a need for revenge.
- A sense that there is no way out; feeling imprisoned in a certain situation.
- A feeling of shame, guilt, and/or anger at oneself.

- A fear of losing control.
- A fear of hurting themselves or hurting others.
- Continuous stress.
- Loss of health (real or imaginary).
- Loss of status, self-esteem, security, and/or money.
- Decline in work or school performance, or in other activities.

References

[1] Hunt, T. Cliffs of Despair: A Journey to the Edge (2006). Random House, Minnesota.

CHAPTER SIX

Suicide Notes

The analysis of suicide notes has been invaluable for specialists all over the word. One could even say that modern suicidology originated from broad research carried out by the American psychologist Dr. Edwin Shneidman, in 1949, on just such letters.

While working at the Brentwood Veterans Hospital in California, Shneidman needed to write condolence messages to two wives who had lost their husbands to suicide, both of whom had been in the hospital. Upon arrival at the coroner's office, he found hundreds of farewell letters that had piled up over the years. "I felt like a Texan millionaire getting home and tripping on a pool of oil," he said about the incident.[1]

Shortly after that, he invited psychologist Norman Farberow to research the letters. Farberow had written his doctorate thesis on suicide attempts in hospitals. Both men were thirty-one years old at the time.

The aim of the study was to find out if there was any pattern in the messages left by those who had completed suicide. With that goal in mind, they created a control group to write fake letters that could be compared with the 721 in possession of the coroner. The researchers wanted to know what they would say to those they left behind. At the end of the study, they drew some very rich conclusions: the 'pseudocides,' a term coined by Shneidman for the invented suicides of the fake letters, did not contain any particular features, as opposed to the actual letters, which followed some patterns, as they had initially predicted.

It was during this period that Shneidman and Dr. Farberow underlined some common characteristics found in suicidal people, among which was ambivalence. Many letters showed that while part of the individual wanted to cease living, there was also a part of them that still wanted to live.

Determined to dive into this theme, they started another study by gathering data from eight thousand people who had killed themselves over a period of ten years. The researchers examined over 200,000 hospital files with names, farewell letters, diaries, and logs of psychological tests and therapy. In partnership with doctors, they gathered data from 501 suicide attempts, and in the halls of the Brentwood Veterans Hospital, they set up a control group for future comparisons.

The findings opened up new perspectives in the field of suicidology. Shneidman and Farberow were able to refute old myths regarding the topic, the first of which was the belief that people who always say they will kill themselves suicide never actually do. They found that the reality was the opposite: 75 percent of the dead had a history of prior attempts, and only 15 percent of them had any sort of psychosis, a finding that contradicted another myth, that only insane people ended their lives.

Nearly half of the people studied had taken their lives within ninety days after an emotional crisis, and they seemed to be recovering at the moment of their deaths. A third of those studied had sought medical help sometime in the six-month period before the suicide, and the vast majority had sent warning signs to family and friends. The researchers concluded that if someone had been able to identify these signs, they might have avoided such tragedies.

They decided to apply their research to help individuals who were at risk of suicide. The researchers phoned Dr. Robert Litman, who had written an article on treating suicidal people in hospitals, and at the time was a director at the Los Angeles Cedars-Sinai Hospital Psychiatry Ward, and they proposed the creation of a Suicide Prevention Center, an innovative initiative in the USA at the time. With financial aid from the National Institute of Mental Health (NIMH), they opened the first such facility in the country, in Los Angeles, in 1958.

Suicidology continued to develop strongly from that point on. Shneidman and Farberow became common reference points in the field. Currently, the USA is the most advanced country in this field of study. A huge part of the concepts used by suicide specialists all over the world came from Shneidman, Litman and Farberow. They defined the warning signs (see Chapter 5) and the measurement of an individual's current lethality (the chances at any point that they will kill themselves in the near future) based on various risk factors. Previously, the standard belief that an individual simply was or was not a suicidal person, as opposed to it being something that could change in either direction over time.

They also created the term 'psychological autopsy,' a *post-mortem* investigation alongside the family and friends of the victim with the aim of reconstructing their mental state at the time of death.

The psychological autopsy was meant to aid the Los Angeles Police Department's investigations in cases where they could not conclude suicide or accident. One of the most famous inquiries conducted by this group was into the death of Marilyn Monroe, due to a barbiturate overdose on August 5, 1962. By interviewing Monroe's family and friends, they learned that she had already tried to kill herself twice before and was going through a depression episode at the time of her death. The conclusion of the investigators was "probable suicide."

What do the letters tell us?

The words present in a suicide note can be indicative of many things. For example, they may reflect events that might have triggered the decision, the emotional and psychological state of the person, or how they want to be perceived by loved ones. A person's suicide note may even include messages to those who will be closely affected by their death. Contrary to popular belief, such notes are rarely present, though there is no consensus in terms of the numbers, and they vary from country to country.

When present, a notable characteristic of these writings is the fact that most of the time, they reveal implicit character traits of the people who wrote them. That was the case with my father. His suicide was carefully planned, which was typical of him. In our family, we used to say that even to do simple things, such as going to the beach, he had to lock down every detail in advance, such as departure and arrival times, etc.

He was a very good strategist, so it was no surprise to see the level of dedication he devoted to the details the planning of his own death. After settling his financial situation (paying debts and closing bank accounts), he wrote two letters: one for when his body was to be found, and the other one sent to me two days before his suicide. It was also important for him that there be no risk of anyone else being held accountable for his death. He stuck the first note on the wall before he pulled the trigger in order to make it clear that it was not a murder, but rather a voluntary death. The note was specifically written for the police—he wanted to avoid an investigation and the unnecessary scrutiny we would have to go through if they opened one. That note was the only one written by hand

and signed. All the other letters had been typed.

My father was never an impulsive man, quite the contrary, so his suicide followed a predictable behavior. This aspect brings me to a very active discussion among specialists—the presence or lack of impulsiveness in suicides. In his book The Suicidal Mind, Shneidman states that "people are very consistent among themselves,"[2] and thus he does not believe that self-inflicted death can be impulsive; he sees it as a continuation of one's usual behavior in life, as well as their usual reactions to pain, loss, threat, and failure.

My father had no internal resources to help him face failure. He tried to go through everything as a superman and as such bore a very hard shell, almost impenetrable. Beneath it, though, his frailty and feelings were numbed by alcohol, which was his way to deal with his struggles and his unexplored—and therefore, unexpressed—self.

On the other hand, he had a family to provide for. We were, in many ways, the sustainers of his life, so when we became independent adults, there was very little left to keep him alive. His three daughters were living far away, his son had passed, and his marriage had recently ended. He lost purpose. In retrospect, at least in this specific case, I agree with Dr. Shneidman in that my father's death was a reiteration of his behavior when alive. He couldn't talk about his pain, he had lost the main drive in his life, and so he had no way out. And as he did in all decisions, he planned the details and executed them, crossing off a checklist.

But it's not always like this. There are no strict formulas for suicide. Three months after my father passed, Alexandrina—one of my closest friends—lost her brother Jose Romero to suicide. He jumped from the twentieth floor of a building, right in front of their sister Celia. At first, the act seemed impulsive to us—we thought the trigger might have been Celia talking with him about the possibility that he would have to take antidepressants for the rest of life, an idea that clearly terrorized him. After Celia confronted him with that, he lost it and jumped from her balcony. At first glance, if we'd heard the story from someone who did not know him well, it would pass as impulsive, but when we carry out a 'psychological autopsy,' it becomes clear that he also followed a pattern congruent with his life story. That's what I attempted to do when I talked to the family.

In an interview with Thomas Joiner, Psychology professor at the University of Florida and author of the book *Why People Commit Suicide*, I asked how he would describe the suicide of Jose Romero, since he agreed with Shneidman's view that impulsiveness is not a prevailing trait in self-inflicted death. Joiner was clear: "The problem with cases such as this is that you can never know what had been in the person's mind days, weeks, and months before their suicide. What happens is that the idea of jumping from a balcony might have been contemplated in the past, but for some reason he left this idea aside. In the moment, he got worse and felt cornered, and he decided to act and jumped. Therefore, the method was not impulsive, although the decision might have been."

He was right. Jose Romero had a history of mental illness and fierce reluctance to follow through with treatment. Starting in adolescence, he had been seen by a variety of different psychiatrists, yet refused to accept the diagnosis of chronic depression, which would mean that he would need to take medication for the rest of his life. In his case, it becomes clear that although the jump may have seemed an impetuous act, it was in fact in line with his lifelong unwillingness to face his illness.

Another important point must be made regarding impulsiveness. Studies[3] show that along with aggressiveness, it plays a greater role in teen suicide, and its role decreases as the age of the person increases. I go into more details on this factor in the Youth chapter.

Not everybody agrees with Shneidman and Joiner, though. The

psychoanalyst Otávio Toledo, who works in São Paulo, Brazil, argues that impulsiveness is in fact present in certain situations: "I believe that there may be impulsiveness in some cases. From my point of view, the psychic functioning is based on polarities: bad and good, passive and aggressive, they are poles of the same matter. Sometimes, the person dives in one pole or the other. The healthy functioning allows for the flow and establishes contact between the two poles when the person is whole. However, in all of us, at some point, there is dissociation and this contact is broken."

Dr. Geraldo Massaro, on the other hand, believes that self-destruction is a human factor, and impulsiveness is a matter related to internal factors:

"The suicide question lies within all of us. Any individual may have, in some capacity, been in touch with it. I believe in the possibility of impulsive suicide, but not like, 'Oh, this is messed up, I'll kill myself.' The contingency exists within the individual; the issues, the self-destructive traits, this dynamic interaction is there. Now, in many cases, had they not had the impulsive factor, they would not have jumped. Denying the impulsiveness is risky, though. I believe that it cannot be reduced to one element, but there are people who indeed kill themselves because of an impulse. It is not that they had never thought about that before and all of a sudden were dead, but there were questions lying within, as we all have inside of us."

The different types of goodbye

The tone of each letter reveals feelings and conflicts that are present during the time of the suicide. Tom Hunt, the author of *Cliffs of Despair*, categorizes four types of tone: accusative, explanatory, practical, and apologetic. With the first, anger is the main drive behind the words. The explanatory type tries to justify the decision, whereas the practical type lists pragmatic measures to be taken after death. The last one comes with a display of empathy for those who are left behind, apologetic about the pain the person is about to inflict.

When the ex-nun Neuza killed herself, she left several notes scattered across her bedroom, one for each sibling and one for her parents. In all of them, she apologized for causing everyone so much pain. At the same time, she attempted to express her feelings, her delusions with life, and the lack of hope that she might get better. According to her sister, Neuza had been diagnosed with depression but refused to undergo treatment. Hers would fall into Hunt's categories of explanatory and apologetic. In my father's case, there was a mix of explanatory ("I can't go on with my present life"), practical (when he explained what to do with his material things), and other elements that do not fit into Tom Hunt's categorization.

The words printed on paper are a sort of mirror that reflects the individual's state of mind. One good example is the suicide note written by the lead singer of Nirvana, Kurt Cobain. He wanted his wife to understand why he was making such a radical choice. The letter was found next to his body on April 8, 1994. Signs of guilt and the total absence of pleasure are recurring themes:

"To Boddah[4],

... I haven't felt the excitement of listening to as well as creating music along with reading and writing for too many years now. I feel guilty beyond words about these things. For example when we're back stage and the lights go out and the manic roar of the crowds begins, it doesn't affect me the way in which it did for Freddie Mercury, who seemed to love, relish in the love and adoration from the crowd which is something I totally admire and envy. The fact is, I can't fool you, any one of you. It simply isn't fair to you or me.

The worst crime I can think of would be to rip people off by faking it and pretending as if I'm having 100% fun. Sometimes I feel as if I should have a punch-in time clock before I walk out on stage. I've tried everything within my power to appreciate it (and I do, God, believe me I do, but it's not enough). I appreciate the fact that I and we have affected and entertained a lot of people. It must be one of those narcissists who only appreciate things when they're gone. I'm too sensitive. I need to be slightly numb in order to regain the enthusiasms I once had as a child. (...) I think I simply love people too much, so much that it makes me feel too fucking sad.

I have a goddess of a wife who sweats ambition and empathy and a daughter who reminds me too much of what I used to be, full of love and joy, kissing every person she meets because everyone is good and will do her no harm. And that terrifies me to the point to where I can barely function. I can't stand the thought of Frances becoming the miserable, self-destructive, death rocker that I've become.

I have it good, very good, and I'm grateful, but since the age of seven, I've become hateful towards all humans in general. Thank you all from the pit of my burning, nauseous stomach for your letters and concern during the past years. I'm too much of an erratic, moody baby! I don't have the passion anymore, and so remember, it's better to burn out than to fade away.

Peace, love, empathy.
Kurt Cobain
Frances and Courtney[5], I'll be at your altar.
Please keep going Courtney, for Frances.
For her life, which will be so much happier without me.
I LOVE YOU, I LOVE YOU!

Unlike Cobain's, the note that the British writer Virginia Woolf left to her husband, Leonard Woolf, on March 28, 1941, did not expose what she was feeling regarding life in general; rather, she zoomed into the exact moment she decided to end it. Woolf also shows altruism, another common underlying theme found in suicidal ideation. Although it sounds unrealistic, many people who attempt or complete suicide truly believe they will improve the lives of their loved ones when they are gone.

In the sweetness of her words, Virginia, taken by the fear of what was coming, expressed all her gratitude to Leonard and detailed the reasoning that led her to suicide:

Dearest,

I feel certain I am going mad again. I feel we can't go through another of those terrible times. And I shan't recover this time. I begin to hear voices, and I can't concentrate. So I am doing what seems the best thing to do. You have given me the greatest possible happiness. You have been in every way all that anyone could be. I don't think two people could have been happier till this terrible disease came. I can't fight any longer. I know that I am spoiling your life, that without me you could work. And you will I know. You see I can't even write this properly. I can't read. What I want to say is I owe all the happiness of my life to you. You have been entirely patient with me and incredibly good. I want to say that - everybody knows it. If anybody could have saved me it would have been you. Everything has gone from me but the certainty of your goodness. I can't go on spoiling your life any longer.

I don't think two people could have been happier than we have been. V."

Another point highlighted by specialists is that goodbyes tend to oscillate between lucidity and complete denial of the reasoning behind the suicide. They may equally be a sign of an acute state of mental confusion. Sometimes, they come in other formats than words, as in the case of the Dutch painter Van Gogh, who shot himself in the chest, on July 27, 1890, amidst a wheat field, in the French village of Auvers-sur-Oise.

Van Gogh had just returned from an asylum in Saint-Rémy, where he had stayed for the treatment of what at the time was called a nervous breakdown. The last picture he painted, Wheatfield with Crows, clearly shows his disturbed psychological state. The intensity of his internal conflicts is represented by the thick layers of paint and the haste of each brushstroke, in the turbulence of the clouds, and in the omnipresent crows, a common omen of death.

Taking the example of Van Gogh, one can see that the form of expression chosen to send a final message has to do with the way in which the individual best communicates with people. It can come in the form of music, literature, drawing, or any other medium that serves as a conduit for emotions. Often, these goodbyes are a desperate plea for help, or are meant to make a statement. An example of the latter happened on July 15, 1974, when the host of the Suncoast Digest TV show, on WXLT-TV, an ABC-affiliated TV station in Florida, shocked viewers by killing herself live on TV. She wanted to let everybody know that she disagreed with the editorial policy adopted by the company.

Christine Chubbuck, twenty-nine years old at the time, suffered from depression and struggled to socialize. Her job was her main source of pleasure. Three weeks before taking her own life, she asked her editor to produce a story on suicide. During the process of creating the story, she interviewed members of the local police department about several aspects of suicide, including the best methods. She was told that the most effective way would be to use a .38-caliber revolver and shoot oneself in the back of the head.

One week before her suicide, she told the evening news editor that she had bought a gun and would kill herself on air, but no one took her seriously. On July 12, she had an argument with her boss because he had replaced one of her stories on suicide with one that covered a gunfight. The owner of the TV station had convinced the team to focus on stories depicting "blood and guts."

On the morning of July 15, 1974, Chubbuck intrigued co-workers by claiming she had to open the show by reading headlines, which was unusual, since it generally always started with an interview. During the first eight minutes of her program, Chubbuck covered three national news stories and a shooting from the previous day at local restaurant. The film reel of the restaurant shooting had jammed and would not run, so Chubbuck shrugged it off and said, on-camera:

> *"In keeping with the Channel 40's policy of bringing you the latest in blood and guts and in living color, you are going to see another first—an attempted suicide."*

Then she drew the revolver and shot herself behind her right ear.

References

[1] Colt, G. (1991). The Enigma of Suicide. New York, NY: Scribner.

[2] Shneidman, E. The Suicidal Mind (1996). Oxford University Press, New York. (reference 44)

[3] Apter A, Gothelf D, Orbach I, Weizman R, Ratzoni G, Har-Even D, Tyano S. (1995). Correlation of suicidal and violent behavior in different diagnostic categories in hospitalized adolescent patients. Journal of the American Academy of Child and Adolescent Psychiatry. 34, 912–918.

[4] Boddah was the name of Kurt's childhood imaginary friend.

[5] His wife Courtney Love.

CHAPTER SEVEN

Those Left Behind

Dealing with death is always a painful experience. For those who lose someone to suicide, several circumstances make it more challenging. Not only is it often sudden, but it's also violent and unexpected. On top of the overwhelming emotions that come with bereavement, when a person takes their own life, they leave behind questions and make room for blaming, guilt, and shame. Suicide is unquestionably one of the most trauma-inducing losses one can endure.

The particularities show up early in the grief process. When a person dies because of an illness or an accident, for example, friends and family show immediate solidarity. They want to know the details of what happened; they speak openly about the situation and offer comfort. Suicide silences people and keeps them at a distance. As a result, those grieving find it hard to search for help. This creates a vicious, destructive cycle that feeds the stigma surrounding voluntary death.

In an article published in the American Journal of Psychiatry, American psychiatrists David Ness and Cynthia Pfeffer conclude that relatives of suicidal people are blamed and avoided more than in other types of death, which increases the tendency for shame, isolation, and self-blame.

The traumas caused by self-inflicted death are also more severe. In his book, *Suicide and Its Aftermath: Understanding and Counselling the Suicide Survivor*, John McIntosh highlights the violent aspect of self-inflicted death:

> *"The strong feelings that are elicited may call forth disturbing and intense thoughts of vengeance and retribution, flooding the survivor with violent images. Family members may feel destructive, lash out at others, and even contemplate taking their own lives."*

He compares the survivors' reactions to those who experienced rape, war, or violent crime. Among the symptoms mentioned are physical numbness, emotional anesthesia, detachment from reality, isolation, loss of interest, and inability to feel emotions, particularly those related to intimacy, sexuality, and tenderness. Other symptoms include difficulty sleeping and staying asleep, lack of concentration, and fear of losing control.

Even when the deceased has had a history of prior attempts or mental disorders, shock is the most common reaction of those affected by suicide. My friend Alexandrina, who lost her twin brother in February 2005, one month after my father killed himself, recalls that his suicide was not necessarily a surprise, but how he did it shocked the family:

> *"The shock was not the death itself, but how it happened. To me, his was an announced death. I knew he would one day complete it, because he had already tried twice before. After he turned forty-five, Maninho (his family nickname) gave signs that his isolation deeply hurt him. Jumping off my sister's balcony was the second tragedy."*

José Romero was forty-five years old when he tried for the first time. On that day, he called his sister Celia, but he couldn't express his feeling over the phone. Later, he arrived "as silent as a grave," as she recalls. It was hard for him to open up. Before anything meaningful had been said, he got up and informed her that he was going back to their parent's home. A few minutes later, Celia received a call from her father saying that José Romero had cut his wrists and been hospitalized.

Alexandrina told me about the time when his problems intensified:

> *"I remember my brother in crisis after the age of forty-four, when life became a bit too challenging for him. Although he had a stable life, with a career and a fully paid condo, José Romero never reached very far. He started his master's degree but did not finish his thesis. He could have lived on his own, but never really got to it. He was very dependent; the day-to-day activities were hard for him. My brother couldn't even turn on a stove. I see his first suicide attempt as his first farewell."*

The second time it happened, José Romero had been diagnosed with depression and showed traces of schizophrenia. After much insistence from Alexandrina, he saw a doctor and started taking the prescribed medication, but he could never accept the diagnosis. The doctor suggested group therapy, but he left the only session he participated in without uttering a single word. In the meantime, he had lost almost forty pounds, but according to his sisters, there were no signs that he had given up. Until the day he made his last visit to Celia:

> *"He had called me five times already. When I got home, I returned his call and invited him over. We started talking about his treatment. Prior to that day, my attitude had always been to reassure him that his illness was temporary, but when he arrived he started telling me that he was going to stop the medication, so I had to take another approach and be firm. I told him that he had to face the reality that he would need his meds for the rest of his life.*

> *His last words were: 'I'm not sick, and I don't want to be drug-dependent.' Then he got up and ran to the balcony. Until that moment, I did not believe he was*

going to do that, but then he climbed on the chair and jumped from the twentieth
floor. I ran screaming and saw that he'd tried to hold onto the wall with his left
hand, a basic human survival instinct, but he slipped and fell to the ground."

The shock that Celia experienced was different from that of the rest of
her family. In addition to the general fact of her brother's brutal death,
she'd witnessed the scene directly, in her own living room, an image that
will stay with her forever. It all happened in less than five minutes—what
seemed to be another casual conversation with José Romero turned his
sister's life upside down. After his death, she was faced with the most
common feeling of those who lose a loved one to suicide: guilt.

What if . . .

It is practically impossible not to question ourselves about what
might have been done to prevent the suicide of someone we know.
This seems to be a natural human reaction. Since I started working with
suicide prevention, I have talked to a large number of people who found
themselves in this situation, and every single one of them invariably
brings up the 'what if' question.

In Celia's case, the possibility of having caused José Romero's death
tortured her for a long time. After the incident on her balcony, she
realized she needed help. For one year, she saw a therapist and took
an antidepressant.

"Now, I talk about his suicide without difficulty. I'm not ashamed to
tell you, just as I'm not ashamed to say he was sick and did not accept his illness.
Sometimes I avoid the issue, so that people don't think that I want them to feel sorry
for me or that I'm trying to show I'm a strong person. They're shocked when they
find out it happened at my house. Usually, the first question they ask is, 'Was he
depressed?' I say yes, since he was sixteen. He had a condo, a job, but he was not

happy. It was not for lack of help, though. I have a clear conscience about that."

Guilt comes in many forms, and it can be directed to anyone: the doctor, who may not have prescribed the appropriate treatment; the spouse, who did not see what was happening; the close friend, who hadn't been around. Anyone is a possible target.

My sister Renata blamed herself for months. Not for my dad's death itself, but for the fact that she had noticed that something was wrong with him but hadn't asked the hard questions. The day before my father's suicide, they met. On several occasions, she had the sense that he planned to kill himself, but she couldn't bring herself to say anything. When she called me crying the next morning, she repeated, insistently, that she had sensed his suicide, but hadn't had the courage to speak.

> *"I felt immense guilt, because he had spent the last day of his life with me. I had a recurrent thought that screamed, 'I knew, I should have done something.' I know it was irrational, of course—after all, what could I have done? Call the police? Call a psychiatrist to commit him to a mental hospital? And say what? 'I think he is going to do something stupid'?"*

Guilt was in my mind as well, because on the last day of my father's life, I had opted not to talk to him on the phone. I believed I would see him in a few days, so I dismissed Renata when she asked me if I want to have a word with him. "Why didn't I talk to dad? Maybe I would have noticed something and could have persuaded him to put the idea aside until I returned home." This was my version of 'what if.'

Blaming others is also inevitable. We experienced it in my family. Aunt Walquiria, my father's closest sister, had a hard time understanding what had happened to him. She needed a scapegoat, which ended up being her own brothers. My sister Renata remembers trying to explain to her that no one was responsible for his death, but to no avail:

"Much of the guilt was directed at their brothers, because they were not close to him. I was with my aunt in Brasilia a few months after his death, and she was furious because, according to her, no one had 'done anything,' and they had 'let him carry out this act of madness.'

She and Uncle Sobrinho (her husband) also extended the grudge to the other brothers, and kept saying that something felt very wrong about it and it had to be someone's fault. As best I could, I told them how my father had lived, his recent struggles, how he dealt with them, and how stressed he had been in the past few months. I do not know if it helped much, but they seemed calmer when I left."

Parents are the most common victims of blame. In addition to the death of the child subverting the natural order of life, they are the ones people point their fingers at when searching for answers. Unfortunately, self-blame is also common. Alexandrina saw it in her parents:

"We didn't tell mom at first, but she got suspiciously curious about the death certificate. I think she knew, otherwise she would not have demanded to see it. The document stated death by heart attack. She would read and ask out loud, 'How can a person die of a heart attack and have a fractured skull?' She got very depressed after that.

My father is stronger, but he had a lot of guilty feelings. Both of them do, and they really shouldn't. When you think about it, at a time when nobody would go to a psychiatrist, they left the countryside and took my brother, at the age of 18, to be treated in Recife. They did what they could, but they still felt guilty. My parents wondered about what they'd wrong. They even questioned why the rest of their kids were successful and he wasn't. The greatest guilt comes from comparing him to us. Where did they fail? That is the lingering question."

Guilt takes many forms. Maxwell, a friend of my family, was alone at home with his father, Max, when he jumped off the building. His dad was a lively, energetic guy, but his life had taken a turn for the worst when he turned forty-five. At the time, he held a high-ranking position in Brazil's largest bank. His job offered him prestige and respect, but he wanted to have his own business, so he left. Things did not turn out as he planned. Maxwell recalls the many barriers his father faced when trying to find his way in the market:

> *"After he left the bank, he received other job offers, but he chose to become a partner in a company that was specializing in the same area as him. Soon, he witnessed corruption and a lot of unethical dealings, so he left. For him, it was a major hit, along with the drop in his professional and financial status. He'd held certain power and autonomy in the bank."*

Gradually, Max's behavior started to change. He became an introverted, sad, pessimistic person. He began treatment for depression, which brought a lot of shame because of the stigma that comes with mental illness. His medication had to be adjusted many times. It got to the point that his wife wouldn't leave him alone anymore for fear that he would hurt himself.

One day, Maxwell went to visit his father in Recife. In the afternoon, while his son took a nap, Max pulled the bed close and jumped through the hole that held the air-conditioning equipment. Maxwell woke up with the insistent ringing of the intercom. Minutes later, he was downstairs, covering his father's body.

Naturally, one would think that Maxwell would blame himself for leaving his father unattended, but that was not the case. Instead, his guilt came from recalling a thought he'd had when seeing his father in a lethargic state: "It's better to die than to live like this." The idea of having "wished" for his father's death haunted him for years. As for his mother, she also experienced guilt for leaving the house that day.

In the case of suicide after a long period of illness, especially a debilitating one that causes much suffering and has no cure, it is natural, at some point, for the family to feel relief after the loved one is gone.

This is another common source of guilt. Regardless of how it shows up, this emotion deserves much attention, because it can grow to the point of taking over one's life, leading to shame and social isolation. I have met many mourners who got stuck in an endless spiral of self-blame that kept them frozen in the past.

Sadness

Unlike other kinds of death, with suicide, sadness often takes longer to show up, because it blends in with the large set of emotions that emerge after this type of loss. Besides the pain of death itself, there is also the need to understand what happened. Suicide shouts the question "Why?" with no guarantee that it will ever be answered.

Amidst the anger, incredulity, and shock, the mourner may find it hard to cry at first. Tears often come in waves. You cry, then you dwell on the 'what ifs' and 'whys'; you blame yourself and others; you feel there is no one to talk to; then you cry again. Your body and mind twirl around in circles of regrets, words unsaid and things you wish could be undone. Your life is put on hold.

After the dust settles, sadness hits you hard. For some people, it may take years, depending on which emotions are in charge. When it comes in full force, knowing the difference between bereavement and depression can be hard, because the line that separates them is quite thin. Mourning is a natural state of dealing with loss, but unlike depression, it fades with time. Depression is the opposite. It grows slowly to the point of robbing you of life's joys. It feels like a mental and physical shutdown. You reach a dead end. That's exactly what happened to me.

In January of 2005, when my dad took his life, I had just moved to São Paulo, in the Southeast of Brazil, to take up a position as the news director of a newspaper. I allowed myself little time for mourning. With the new job came huge responsibilities and long workdays. In addition, I knew practically no one in that city and was far from my family and friends. In hindsight, I see that I camouflaged the pain by occupying every minute of my day. Apart from work, I registered in countless online courses, did regular exercise, and left no time for grieving.

A few months later, I began to feel that there was something wrong with me. I had no energy, took no pleasure in the things I used to love, and had zero interest in meeting people. I felt tired most of the time and started having bouts of crying. Being a very rational person, I would find justifications for everything—after all, I was in a city that is famous for overwhelming people with its population of twelve million, its noisy streets and almost-complete lack of green areas.

Months went by, and I kept getting worse. I remember having lunch with my younger sister, Eveline, during which I told her I was not well. The second those words came out of my mouth I burst into tears. Knowing me and how rare it was to see me cry, she told me straight away, "Please get some help, you seem really unwell."

It took me a couple of years to follow her advice. Before that, one by one, I solved all the problems that could be causing my sadness. The first thing to do was my job. In June 2007, I resigned. Then, I bought a condo in a neighborhood of São Paulo where I had many friends. Nothing helped, so I decided to see a psychiatrist.

The final straw came in October 2007, during a trip to visit a friend in New York. Few things bring me as much joy as traveling, but that trip was a nightmare. I felt confused and distracted, and more than anything, total apathy to what was happening around me. All I could think about was coming home. At night, I would hide in my room and cry. That was the proof I needed to search for medical help.

I got home on a Friday. Over the weekend, I could hardly get out of bed.

On Sunday, I wrote an email to one of the psychiatrists I had interviewed for this book, asking for an emergency appointment. One day later, they diagnosed me with depression. The mourning I had not allowed myself to process had finally caught up with me.

One of the women I talked to while researching suicide grief told me a similar story. Neide, who also lived in São Paulo at the time, lost her oldest sister Neuza in 1998. They had been raised by strict parents in a large family of eight. According to Neide, Neuza was like a second mother to them. She was loving and present, always with a smile on her face. Neuza had many friends and seemed to lead a happy life. But her inner world was a different story.

At age fifteen, she decided to be a nun and went to live in a convent, which had always been her childhood dream. Neuza believed that by doing so, she would be able to devote her life to helping the poor communities of Marília, her hometown. Very early on, she became disappointed with her choice and began to have bouts of depression. She also missed her family. One time, when talking to her siblings, she revealed her frustration: "Here, if people in need knock on the door, they tell us to close it, to keep them out or say there is no one here." She kept changing congregations in search of what she wanted, but never found it.

After returning to Marília, Neuza stayed at the home of a bishop, where she did housework and began to study psychology, but soon the church stopped paying for her studies, so she had to request a leave of absence. Her mental state continued to decline. During a visit from her family, the bishop arrived home and asked everyone to leave. For her, that was the last straw, as her sister Neide remembers:

> "She cried a lot, and I said to her, 'If you do not leave, we'll have to get you out of here. You cannot stay this way.' She had lost a lot of weight; her

suffering was visible. She kept saying, 'I did not leave my whole family to wash someone else's floors. I want to help people.'"

Neuza finally moved back home, which was a breath of fresh air. She took a university entrance exam at her state university and came in fourth place, but the academic environment led to another crisis. She believed she was not able to meet the demands of the university. At this time, she decided to take her own life.

Soon after leaving the convent, at the age of twenty-eight, Neuza had gone to the doctor and left with the diagnosis of depression. According to her sister, she never took the prescribed pills. She confided in Neide that she'd been aware of having the illness, which she called "the cancer of the soul," since she was fifteen years old. In Neide's recollections, however, her predisposition was clear even earlier, from childhood:

"As a child, she would lock herself in the bathroom and cry. I was very attached to her, and these images are strong in my memory. I remember my mother asking, 'What is the matter, Neuza?' And she would answer 'nothing.' I always saw her like this, and she could never say why."

The last conversation she had with Neuza was in June, when Neide revealed to the family that she was pregnant. Her sister was very pleased. The following month, Neide went to Marília to visit them, and Neuza told her, "I am so happy for you. A child is a blessing. I will not have that blessing." Today, she sees clearly that her sister's words were warning signs indicating that she had decided to die.

All the medication prescribed by her doctor was used for the suicide. Beside the body, they found several boxes of antidepressants, the ones that Neuza had refused to take for months. Throughout the room, there were flowers and letters addressed to each member of the family. Due to her pregnancy, Neide suppressed the pain of the loss, in fear of harming the baby. After childbirth, she plunged into the tasks of motherhood, continuing to postpone that mourning:

"Now I go to Marília, I visit her tomb, I cry, I talk to her. But at the time, I couldn't even think about her. I also didn't dream about my sister. Now I have flashbacks. Sometimes I play videos of us to remind me of the good memories. For a long time, I blocked all of it, because I couldn't accept what she had done. The thought would come, and I would repress it. When I was breastfeeding, I avoided these images."

In the case of Alberto, a forty-nine-year-old Brazilian from São Paulo, the effects of suppressing his pain took almost three decades to manifest. When his father killed himself at forty-two, Alberto was a teenager. It happened after his dad was fired from a factory where he had worked for seventeen years. He was ashamed of the situation, and moved away from his family, falling into depression.

"After being let go, he tried to pick himself up. He opened a small bar, but we started noticing that he was not the same. He wouldn't sleep and would walk aimlessly around the house. We could see his shame, as if everything had been his fault. He smoked a lot. The bar was his last resort. I could tell that he was worn out, but I did not know why or what to do. My mother once told me, 'Your father is not well, we have to keep an eye on him. He could do something stupid.'"

He never accepted what had happened; he saw it as a personal failure. Back then, no one sought psychological help or even medication. After his death, I felt as if there was something wrong with us, because suicide was not a common thing. Somehow, it made me feel inferior. When people asked about his death, I used to say he'd had a heart attack." Like in the other situations related here, his father had also given clear signs of what he was planning to do. In late 1975, he called Alberto and said, "Son, you're the oldest. If I ever falter, you need to take care of your mother and your siblings."

Alberto's answer was, "I'm going to do what a sixteen-year-old can do, but you're not going to be absent, that doesn't make sense."

His father simply responded, "Son, I could suddenly be gone."

His death came in January 1976, turning the family's lives upside down, particularly that of Alberto, who became responsible for providing for the rest of them. They had to move to a tiny house that didn't even have a private bathroom:

"My mother turned inward and became a mournful person, as if she had lost the right to happiness. Women of that time were bred to have husbands and children, and be happy with that. She had to work. It was a painful process. We did not have money to pay the rent. I went to school during the day and worked at night, and so did my brother. Just so you get a clear idea of it, our biggest dream was to live in a house with a bathroom."

In his busy routine, Alberto had no time to internally process his father's death, nor their conversation from shortly before the suicide. The impact of repressing his grief came to a head in 2000:

"I began to feel a relentless sadness but thought it was because of work. That's when I decided to seek therapeutic help. I went to treatment for two years, during which I finally processed my losses. I unraveled everything that had been locked inside of me for almost thirty years. I cried more than I could ever have thought possible. My therapist said, 'You need to admit that he has done you harm. You always thought of him as a victim, but it was you and your brother who were hurt. If you don't face that, you will suffer.'"

Anger

Anger is a secondary emotion. We tend to resort to it in order to protect ourselves from the real feelings we are trying to cover up. In the face of suicide, anger radiates in all directions, particularly at the deceased. It is a contradictory reaction: we cry for the person who is gone, but at the same time, we get angry at the person who caused their death.

Spouses are notably struck by anger because of the pain and trauma they see inflicted in their children. I remember a woman I talked to, whose husband had died more than twenty years prior to the interview, and who was still angry at him. She blamed her husband for her oldest daughter's behavioral problems. The child had been the one who found him dead in the bathroom. For the woman, the death of her husband had been an act of selfishness, cowardice, and total disregard for the family.

Every time I talk to a grieving family member, I often ask whether or not anger has been part of their mourning. Alexandrina said that she felt her brother had no right to put her parents through such pain. He should have thought of those who loved him. In addition, the fact of being a twin added what she calls the loss "of my other half."

Maxwell did not get angry, but he remembers that his mother felt hatred for her husband for several years:

> *"She said that he had abandoned his children. I talked to her, tried to explain that it was an extreme situation, that no one wants to take their own life, and that for that to happen something must be terribly wrong."*

Alberto's answer to my question was, "His problem was 'solved,' but what about ours?"

During therapy, he went through the ritual of 'burying' his father. As part of this process, he had to let out his frustrations and anger toward him— Alberto had been forced to fulfill the role of provider and had lost his youth in the meantime. Who was responsible for that radical change? His father. The anger had to be externalized so that he could be healed.

My sister Renata had her moments of anger as well. One time, in a restaurant, a song that reminded us of my father started playing. She looked at me with watery eyes and said quietly, "Sometimes, I feel so angry at him."

My younger sister Eveline was angry at the fact that he had killed himself at home, which led to his wife finding his body in the bedroom. "He shouldn't have made his wife witness and live that horror."

I never felt that anger. For many years, I wondered about what it meant, why I didn't feel angry. I worried about it. Was it denial? Would it come back to haunt me? I thought everybody must feel it at one time or another, but it just never happened to me. Again, grief is an individual journey. There is no right and wrong when it comes to bereavement.

Fear of genetic inheritance

Will I ever kill myself? That question, to one degree or another, haunts many of us survivors. Apart from the fact that suicide reminds us of our own mortality, it carries the fear of a genetic predisposition to voluntary death. I remember Renata's worst depressive phase, when she confided in me that she was afraid to "end up like him." In her case, it was ultimately a positive feeling, because it worked as an incentive to seek treatment. By choosing to bravely face her fears, my sister chose to embrace life.

There is no denying that, after my father's death, we became more watchful with each other. When Renata was depressed, we talked daily. I wanted to keep track of what was going on with her so that, at the slightest sign of something more serious, I would have time to intervene. She did the same during my own depression. When I wrote an email to my sisters about my diagnosis, Renata immediately called me, in tears. It was as if she was reliving her own experience. I asked her to stop crying, even joking that I was the one depressed, not her. Her response was, "But it's very sad to know that you are going through this, and you know that, because you experienced the same with me." From then on, she started to call every day.

Eveline wanted me to move in with her for a while. That same week, she came to São Paulo for a visit. Fortunately, in times of crisis, my sisters and I have a strong sense of humor. We often laugh at the most tragic situations. In our family, one of our aunts used to call us a "closed condominium." If you were not a member, you could only enter with permission.

Her statement was a reference to how close we've always been as sisters. After my diagnosis, we decided to "adopt" depression as the "condo disease." I joked with Eveline, saying that her turn would probably come, but at least we already knew which meds would be most effective.

Alberto's brother was afraid of his DNA as well. During tough times, he thought about taking his own life, which was revealed to Alberto in a letter:

"He never talked much about it with me. In the letter, he warned me: 'It's not worth it.' He said, 'I was close to committing suicide, but today I know it would have been a waste. I would have missed so much.' He did not directly say, 'Don't do it,' but rather, 'My dear brother, we will be together in good and bad times, but we will not give in.' I keep his letter to this day."

After the death of her brother, Celia confesses to having caught herself staring at her balcony and thinking: "Would I ever do something like this? But then I say, 'Forget it.' I'm not afraid of dying, but to do this? No way. I've already been told to put up a screen around the apartment, but I refuse to do it. I am a positive and optimistic person, and I have a lot of faith."

Maxwell's brothers were concerned about him for a while, because he had been the one person at home when it happened. One day, his oldest brother, Junior, talked to him and said he also feared for himself. As for Neide, she keeps a close eye on her siblings: "We have a family history, and we need to stay alert."

The stigma

It was suicide. He killed himself. He took his own life. Whichever way you put it, answering the question "How did he die?" causes an immediate discomfort for those around you. There is no escape from it. Nobody expects this answer, and they react in many ways. The most common is to change the subject and ignore what was just said. Renata sums it up well:

> *"I never lied, I don't feel the need to, but there is a stigma—people totally change after they ask, 'Died of what?' and you answer with the truth. It is as if they're outraged that you put them in such an unpleasant situation. It's even funny sometimes. No one acts normally afterward. Once they hear suicide, they end the conversation—no more questions are asked, and they act as if nothing had happened."*

Unfortunately, part of the reason behind the silence is the fact that suicide is still taboo. People don't know how to handle voluntary death. Those who understand a little of this process may ask if the family member was depressed, if they had problems, yet even so, they often make the mistake of thinking there must have been a specific reason for the act.

It is never that simple. If you investigate further, you will most certainly find a combination of factors that help explain what happened. There may be a specific trigger, but there is rarely a single reason.

Changing the subject may be annoying, but some people have much worse reactions. A few days after my father's death, a woman asked my younger sister what he had died from. When she heard the word suicide, she looked at Eveline and said, "Your father is in a horrible place, and he will suffer to get out of there."

Maxwell faced something similar. When replying to a co-worker that his father had taken his life, she questioned him, in an angry tone of voice, "Why on earth did you say that?" to which he replied, "Because you asked." She didn't stop there, berating him, "You could have said it was an accident or something."

How to tell a child

This is one of the hardest tasks. We fear that by talking to an impressionable child about suicide, we may send the dangerous message that taking one's life is somehow okay, that it is an option when faced with adversities. The future impact on the child is our main concern. Experts argue that the best way to deal with the situation is to be honest, which may avoid future trauma when the truth inevitably comes out.

One expert suggestion is to explain that self-inflicted death is not a natural fact of life, and that the person who did it was not well, which caused them to carry out the suicide. They also recommend to point out that in cases of mental illness, treatments are the best course of action. Each case has its specificities, and those varied circumstances should be brought into the conversation.

Another important point is to try to identify if the child expresses any signs of guilt about the death. Children often do, and if that's the case, you can assure them that it's not true, that they were not responsible for what happened. Make yourself available to talk to them about their feelings, and make sure to maintain their routine.

CHAPTER EIGHT

How To Treat Suicide Grief

A guide for therapists

Miguel was born into a wealthy, well-known Brazilian family. Although the town where he lived has over 350,000 inhabitants, Franca still feels like a small city, where everybody knows everybody and news travels fast. In July 2016, when the local radio station announced his death by suicide, the city was shocked. No one could believe that a successful businessman, a father of four kids—one still a toddler—and an example of philanthropy could be anything short of fulfilled and happy. He had been known for his charity work, for being the life of the party, dedicated to those he loved, and hardworking. But, as happens with all of us, there was more to him than what he externalized. That, unfortunately, turned out to be more than he could bear.

In order to understand the context of his death, I interviewed his ex-wife and his three adult daughters: Isabela, Ana Paula, and Gabriela. All of them talked about Miguel with love, yearning, and serenity. The girls hold onto the positive traits of him as a father, and I could tell from their words that he was truly loving and present in their lives. They all expressed immense, almost palpable sadness. Seldom have I seen a family so dedicated to protecting each other, so honest and emotionally aware of the events that pushed their loved one to despair.

At times, they moved me to tears—maybe because I identified with them. After all, we had so much in common: like mine, their father Miguel had been on his second marriage, had three daughters and one younger son, and experienced an immense sense of failure at 'not being enough.' The children, like my siblings and me, tried to help in the last years of his life, and in the end, his death was followed by the endless 'whys' that haunt us all after a suicide.

Miguel was the oldest of four. His family owned the largest shoe store and distributor chain in Brazil. Very early on, he knew he would take on the business, which he did as a young man. In his early twenties, he suffered a painful loss—his brother, who was one year younger, killed himself in the same way Miguel would decades later. The shock of his brother's death was intensified by the fact that his parents remained silent about it. His mother fell into despair and was never the same again; the grief they all felt was muffled by shame. Even later in life, when Miguel's kids asked him about their uncle, he would change the subject. It was a forbidden topic in the family.

In his early forties, after a succession of economic crises in Brazil and increased competition with Chinese products, the business he headed filed for reorganization bankruptcy. Over the following ten years, he would work endless hours trying to save the family business. Gabriela, his oldest, worked in the factory with him, and remembers that period well.

"He took over, sold a lot of assets, and paid most of the debts, and when the situation improved, the family members decided to participate in the decision-making. It was so much pressure. We started asking him to leave, to try something else. After all, he had been working there since he was twelve years old!"

By the time he declared bankruptcy, he had already been divorced from his first wife for a few years and had recently married one of the company's lawyers. After the family's heirs took over, he felt left out and fell into depression.

"Suddenly, he couldn't make decisions anymore, so he began to consider leaving it altogether. It was very hard for him; the company was his life. At times, he couldn't even get out of bed, couldn't go to work anymore," recalls Ana Paula, his middle child. His kids and wife wanted him out.

The decision to leave was a painful one, and what seemed to be a chance to rebuild his life left him even more depressed. He would call the girls and complain of having nothing to do. They would try to cheer him up, to show him options, very much like my sisters and I did for our father. Ironically, that inversion of roles would make him feel even worse. Aren't fathers supposed to do that for their kids?

"He felt empty, useless, since his agenda was empty for the first time in his life. I saw my dad change dramatically. He would worry about everything: money, the political situation in Brazil, everything! I would ask, 'Dad, what happened? You've always been an optimist,'" Ana Paula told me.

His second marriage was falling apart, and he had moved out of the house. During this period, he attempted suicide twice. After one of these attempts, Isabela remembers telling him, "You can't do this—you will destroy us, Dad."

Days before his death, Miguel stayed with Gabriela. He was thin, sad, and barely speaking. For hours at a time, he would stay on the sofa. Sometimes, he would say, "I'm causing you all too much trouble, I'm worrying everybody; I don't want to be a burden. I don't want this anymore. I need to leave for your own good." On a daily basis, the daughters would talk on the phone, trying to find a way to help him, but nothing seemed to work.

Miguel was taking medication, which stabilized him temporarily, but his mood would alternate between incapacitating depression and manic episodes accompanied by euphoria and restlessness. At the time, he was seeing a psychiatrist who was also functioning as his therapist.

One day, the therapist called Ana Paula and asked her to participate in the next session with her father. His "diagnosis" was short, dry, and judgmental—certainly one of the worst cases of abuse of power I've heard in my years of experience dealing with bereaved families.

The therapist looked at Miguel's daughter and said:

> *"You know what the problem with your father is? He was born with a silver spoon in his mouth. I know his family; he has always been spoiled and pampered, and he lacks humility. So, he's been saying that he will kill himself? He might, and you know what will happen if he does? His son, your brother, will be mentally ill just like him. He will be traumatized and may even do the same in the future."*

As she was telling me this, I sensed resentment in Ana Paula's words, but what upset me the most was her naïve demeanor. To this day, she still questions whether or not the doctor had good intentions when he laid out her father's ominous "prognosis" in front of him.

"Maybe he wanted to shock my dad, so that he would react?" she asked me.

I wanted to shout, "What? Sue him!" but I knew better, and just listened. It was hard to keep myself impartial, but I followed a motto I often repeat to myself: in a hopelessly bad situation, if you can't say something positive, something helpful, don't say anything at all. So I remained silent in deference to her grief.

Immediately after the session, the doctor told them he could no longer treat Miguel, alleging he knew the family too well. That was what Ana

Paula said. Isabela told me another version, that the doctor had said that he wouldn't see him anymore because he was sure he would end up killing himself. Either way, it was equally unethical, showing a total lack of compassion, commitment, and empathy toward the patient.

The family searched for another physician. Ana Paula recalls that her father—who at the time was trying all kinds of interventions in order to get better—questioned the new psychiatrist about if meditation would help. His reply was, "If you are not born a Buddha, you will never be a Buddha," totally discrediting meditation as a form of therapeutic practice.

But the sequence of bad counseling they experienced doesn't end there. After her father's death, Isabela went back to see another counselor, someone she had seen previously. When I asked her if therapy helped with her grief process, she said, "I didn't really talk about it, because it upset her too much. The first thing she told me when I came back was, 'He couldn't have done this to you, you were his daughter!' She was angry and blamed my father's new wife for his death.'"

So Isabela decided not to touch on the subject of her father's suicide; it was clearly something to be avoided. In other words, she went to counseling to work through her loss, but didn't feel comfortable talking about it due to the therapist's emotional reaction.

Although quite extreme, these accounts demonstrate our responsibility as mental health professionals. They illustrate the impact we can have on our clients and, most of all, how our own values and beliefs can negatively interfere with our work. In this chapter, I hope to help therapists, both new and experienced, to reflect on what we can do to sit alongside our patients through their grief, particularly grief around suicide, with respect for their uniqueness and their losses, and with compassion for their pain.

The popularized phases of grief

When, in 1969, Elisabeth Kübler-Ross wrote her observations of how terminally ill patients reacted to their imminent deaths, she had no idea that they would quickly become well-known all over the world, and be considered scientific findings, or a "model," as some clinicians call them. The first time I heard about denial, anger, bargaining, depression, and acceptance was over a decade ago, when I was watching "Separações" (*Separations*), one of my favorite Brazilian movies. In the opening scene, the main protagonist starts a conversation with his friends, citing Kübler-Ross's phases. This demonstrates just how widespread her theory became.

What many people fail to understand is that Kübler-Ross's phases were never about grief as a result of losing someone we love. Her professional experience as a clinician was to treat patients on their deathbed; therefore, what she witnessed and later wrote about was the most common stages the patients went through when facing their own death, not somebody else's. Also, she never proclaimed these stages were scientific. Her considerations were based on individual anecdotes that she collected over years of experience. In the first pages of her book, *On Death and Dying*, where the famous phases come from, she made this very clear:

> *"In the following pages is an attempt to summarize what we have learned from our dying patients in terms of coping mechanisms at the time of terminal illness. . . . I have worked with the dying patients for the past two-and-a half years and this book will tell about the beginning of this experiment. . . . It is not meant to be a textbook on how to manage dying patients, nor is it intended as a complete study of the psychology of the dying."*

If we look at the phases themselves, it becomes clear that one of them—bargaining—doesn't even make sense when you apply it to grieving the death of a loved one. What could we bargain for if the person is already gone? When applied to the population she referred to, it certainly rings true though. According to Ruth Davis Konigsberg, a senior editor at TIME magazine and author of the book *The Truth About Grief*, Kübler-Ross, acknowledging the impact of her book worldwide, even thought about changing the title "stages" to "responses." However, she left the original idea untouched, because it had become "ingrained in the culture."

Ruth theorizes that people insist on "stages" as an attempt to bring order to grief's contradictions. She explains, "We accept it in order to reach goals. It turns a complicated experience into an orderly, predictable progression."

Kübler-Ross tried to correct this many times in interviews and writings. In *On Grief and Grieving*, published in 2005, she and her co-author, David Kessler, changed "phases of grief" to "phases of loss," and again tried to rectify what had been misused over time:

> *"The stages have evolved since their introduction and they have been very misunderstood over the last few decades. They were never meant to help tuck messy emotions into neat packages. They are responses to loss that many people have, but they are not a typical response to loss as there is no typical loss. Our grief is as individual as our lives.*
>
> *They are not stops on some linear timeline in grief. Not everyone goes through all of them or goes in a prescribed order."*

Most authors who write about grief emphasize the fact that when it comes to bereavement, although some feelings such as anger, sadness, shock, and denial may be often present, the attempt to categorize them may be harmful to the patient. Actually, Kübler-Ross's phases are so widespread that sometimes clients will come to therapy specifically because they were expecting to follow the linear path of the five stages. If one is not present, they suspect that there is something wrong with them. When this happens, Tamara Cobb, a counselor specializing in traumatic bereavement, tries to educate her patients. "I tend to alert them about the abuse of this notion," she explains. "The problem is that people measure themselves according to it, and when they don't experience the phases, they become confused. 'Am I grieving the wrong way?' they ask."

Dr. Jami Howell, who does grief therapy in Portland, Oregon, agrees: "They get frustrated, because they are not moving quickly enough. 'Why am I not sad, but numb?' is something I hear in my office."

Dr. Rand Michael pointed out an interesting way of looking at this. He takes an integrated approach to counseling, combining different theoretical frameworks with new advances in interpersonal neuroscience. This approach has been revolutionizing the field. He believes that when it comes to grief, the idea of stages places us in a sequential order, which may give the client the impression—and feelings associated with it—that they will be moving away from the deceased. In order to avoid that, he takes a circular approach, where the loss is placed in the middle.

"We relate to it differently over time," he says. "Any aspect of the grief is in the background, even though some are more predominant at times. It's not an either/or phase."

Dr. Brian Goff, a clinical psychologist in Portland, provided me with another simple view of the same issue.

> "The belief of a linear path is a myth. It looks more like facets of grief, not stages; facets of the process. You move in and out of them, you move forward a couple of steps and back. The patient may revisit one expression of grief many times, even though they did it already. They may visit anger, touch on acceptance, but, when there's a bump in the road, be reminded of something and then go back to 'if only, what if?' over and over again."

I would add that not only do we experience feelings in a cyclical fashion, but very often they overlap. Being angry, for example, doesn't rule out guilt and sadness. This is actually one of the most common sources of mental exhaustion for the bereaved: feeling overwhelmed by emotions that at many times are contradictory.

One of the ways the concept of phases may be used was described to me by Henry Cameron, a counselor who spends most of his time working with crisis and loss. If he finds that the patient is having a hard time naming their emotions, to facilitate the process, he may bring up stages of grief. "In our culture, people want guidelines, but I make sure they know that it can happen in any order and come back. For me, it's just a way to frame it." In his experience, this approach has been positive. "Clients feel that I am willing to talk about the ambiguity of death."

Tracy Sandor, a counselor who works with trauma in Portland, Oregon, agrees that sometimes using Küble-Ross's phases may help initialize therapy. "It is a way to help them give language to their feelings," she says, but adds that she always makes sure that patients understand that there are no set paths, no right and wrong. "I tell them that wherever they are is where they are supposed to be … that those are some of the stages some people feel, but they are not linear. Everything psychological follows no regular trajectory. It is individual."

Dr. William Worden's tasks of mourning

Dr. William Worden's book, *Grief Counseling and Grief Therapy*, is quite popular among mental health professionals, and for good reasons. He offers us a comprehensive view on grief therapy, with valuable tips on human reactions to specific types of grief. He discusses what to expect in terms of behavior, cognition, and psychological pain, as well as what to look for when assessing patients and how to facilitate mourning. He also provides useful techniques to be applied during therapy. It is a priceless reference to have at hand. Worden covers a wide range of issues related to the subject, but is best known for his "tasks of mourning." Before we direct our attention to suicide bereavement, I believe it is relevant to look at these tasks.

The 4th and latest edition of *Grief Counseling* and *Grief Therapy* comes with significant changes in the tasks, particularly the fourth one. These shifts were necessary not only to update the content to be in line with theoretical developments in the field, but also because his words gave the mourner the idea that they would need to forget the deceased. This caused discomfort and pain for some patients. His tasks are very different from Kübler-Ross's, because they are proactive, instead of passive and focused on emotions. They direct therapy towards specific achievements so that a person can be functional and move forward with life. Worden also explains that they are not always linear and can be rearranged according to the client's individual path.

The first task is "To accept the reality of loss," which relates to helping the patient face the finality of death. This idea is quite useful when denial takes form. Some examples of denial are delusions, mummification of possessions—rooms that are kept untouched, waiting for the deceased to use them—pretending the person is still alive, or even diminishing the meaning of the loss with statements such as, "He was not that close to me." If the mourner holds on too tightly to material things that belonged to the deceased, this may symbolize their incapacity to acknowledge the immutability of the separation.

Some of these concepts may sound extreme, but denial does happen. Leslie Storm, one of the therapists I interviewed, has worked with grief most of her life and facilitates a suicide support group in Portland. She lost her husband to suicide in 1987.

"For one year, I thought he was on a business trip. Did I believe it? No, but I clung to it. At the end of the year, I said to myself, 'You better wake up, he is not on a business trip,'" she recalls.

The next step is to "Process the pain." Worden posits that the longer a griever avoids the emotions associated with the loss of a loved one, the longer the pain will last. Negation of feelings may take many forms. The patient may avoid thinking about the deceased, overwork, engage in multiple activities in order to avoid solitude, or even self-medicate with drugs and alcohol.

Idealizing the dead is another form of negation, because it will stop the bereaved from facing ambiguities and the wholeness of not only the dead person, but also the relationship they shared. An abusive father, for example, may be portrayed as the perfect caregiver. Worden cites the British psychiatrist John Bowlby, well-known for his revolutionary theory of attachment, who said, "Sooner or later, some of those who avoid all conscious grieving break down—usually with some form of depression."

In her book, *Grief Works: Stories of Life, Death and Surviving,* Julia Samuel, who has been working with the bereaved for almost three decades, emphasizes the need to process the pain cause by the death of a loved one.

"Contrary to all our instincts, to heal our grief, we need to allow ourselves to feel the pain. We need to find ways to support ourselves in it for it cannot be escaped. The paradox of grief is that finding a way to live with the pain is what enables us to heal . . . pain is the agent of change."

Worden's third task is "To adjust to a world without the deceased," which is divided into external, internal, and spiritual. This may be a long process, because it involves not just the individual, but the whole family system. The death of a father, for example, will demand changes in the relationships of the siblings as well. The older brother or sister may have to take on responsibilities that were not expected of them before. The wife will probably need to learn new skills due to the natural assignment of tasks that a couple agrees on when running a household. Even identifying what roles the individual played may be a long process. The third task may vary from person to person; it will largely depend on the relationship with the deceased.

When it comes to internal adjustments, the author refers to how the loss impacts one's sense of self. If the relationship was strongly enmeshed, for instance, adapting may take longer and be more difficult. The level of dependence on each other is one of the aspects to consider. Self-esteem and self-efficacy are very important as well, because they are central to a person's belief that they can move forward on their own. In his article, "Continuing Bonds and Adjustment at 5 years after the Death of a Spouse," Dr. George Bonanno, professor of clinical psychology at Teachers College, Columbia University, concludes that excessive dependency has a direct influence on one's bereavement:

"However, bereaved individuals who were overly dependent on their spouse in the past relationship are more likely to make excessive use of such (continuing bond) expressions well after the death, given their greater difficulty accepting the permanence of the loss."

In his book, *The Other Side of Sadness: What the New Science of Bereavement tells Us About Life After Loss*, Bonanno also clarifies that there are no conclusive findings regarding the healthy or maladaptive nature of maintaining bonds to the deceased. The author invites us to consider what he calls "moderating variables," which means that the act of holding onto possessions, for example, cannot be examined in a vacuum. Keeping an object is different from maintaining the deceased's personal belongings exactly as they were prior to death.

"This behavior becomes obsessive: there is only one way a room can be arranged; there is only one place this or that object can go — where he had it, the way

she would have wanted it. We can see intuitively that there is something wrong here."

Bonanno cites three factors to consider when evaluating whether or not the bond is a healthy one: time, the intensity of the bond, and the quality of attachment with the deceased.

William Worden's fourth task was modified twice. It started as, "Emotionally withdrawing energy from the deceased and reinvesting it in another relationship." Then it became, "Emotionally relocate the deceased and move on with life." Finally, the latest version changed again: "To find enduring connection with the deceased in the midst of embarking on a new life."

The alteration was significant, because the prior options were often interpreted as moving away from the deceased. The idea met with resistance, because mourners and clinicians frowned upon the concept of "breaking up" the relationship. It made some patients feel that they were dishonoring their loved one. Worden recognized that the dead are never totally forgotten, so counselors should be mindful when addressing this issue in order to "find appropriate place for the dead in their emotional lives." The idea is to foster continuing bonds with loved ones while building a new life without them.

An important point must be made regarding Worden's last task. He affirms that when talking about the process of grief, one should avoid words like "closure" and "recovery." He believes that "adaptation" is preferable. Other authors posit the same.

In his book, *Getting Grief Right: Finding your Story of Love in the Sorrow of Loss*, Dr. Patrick O'Malley talks about his own questions regarding grief after he lost his infant son. Being a psychologist himself, he took on new approaches to bereavement after going through loss. One of his conclusions was specifically regarding the final goal of therapy and is closely related to Worden's fourth task. Dr. Patrick believes that the shift he made in his clinic work had a powerful impact on his patients:

"When closure or resolution was no longer the goal, when clients were convinced they were not getting their grief wrong, their need for therapy abated or disappeared altogether.

My practice thus evolved from one of a grieving therapist who promoted modern grief theories to one of a grieving therapist/companion/listener/story encourager . . . my clients and I redefined the nature of 'successful' grieving.

Grief wasn't getting over loss; it was learning to live with it and to use the grief narrative as a way to preserve the bond with the one who died."

In one of the most moving passages of his book, O'Malley re-signifies the suffering of his clients, connecting the pain they feel to their relationship with the deceased:

"They come to understand that their grief was a function of their love."

Dr. Brian Goff said something similar and equally meaningful to me during interview:

"You only hurt about the things you care about . . . as painful as it is, it's a window into your values. Find someone who doesn't hurt, and this is somebody who doesn't care."

The concept of continuing bonds requires further examination. Worden defines them as "attachments to the deceased that are maintained rather than relinquished." He recognizes that the impact of keeping this connection, as well as the types of bond nurtured by mourners, still needs to be researched.

Four questions are central to what needs to be considered by a therapist: What kind of bonds can be helpful with adapting to the loss? Who benefits from these bonds? In what timeframe are they more or less adaptive? Closer to the death or farther from the loss? The last consideration to be made is the impact of culture and religion on maintaining healthy bonds.

Worden's discussion on continuing bonds is a valid one that needs to be taken into account during treatment. It seems that finding a balance between building a fulfilling future and preserving part of the relationship alive is a good way to honor the severed connection. After all, what the patient shared is not only a significant piece of their past, but more importantly, a piece of the mosaic of their lives and who they are.

Kübler-Ross's stages and Worden's tasks are by no means the only references on the subject. In the 1970s, the British psychiatrists Colin Murray Parkes and John Bowlby defined four phases of mourning: shock and numbness, yearning and searching, disorganization and despair, and reorganization and recovery. We also have George Engels's six stages: shock and disbelief, developing awareness, restitution, resolving the loss, idealization, and outcome. In the late 1980s, Catherine Sanders's five phases of bereavement were developed: shock, awareness of loss, conservation withdrawal, healing, and renewal.

The reason why I chose to examine Kübler-Ross and Worden's contributions in more detail was due to the popularity and misuse of Elisabeth's phases, and the value of Worden's ideas. His approach is less about what happens to someone, and more about what can be done to help clients move forward with their lives. Worden's ideas were specifically developed for therapists. He brings up important concepts and goals for us to keep in mind. Again, not as a 1-2-3, static, linear, invariable set of steps, but as mental notes we can aim to use to help our patients through their individual journeys.

Is suicide bereavement different?

When researching for this chapter, I asked this question to all the twenty psychologists and counselors I interviewed. Although I had read several books and articles on grief, some of them specific to suicide, I needed to make sure I was not letting my own experience contaminate my writing. When confronted with this reflection, all of them said "yes." Each one would highlight a few reasons why they believed it to be unique, and most of them mentioned guilt, the "why question," the never knowing, and the stigma surrounding voluntary death.

In 2005, Jacqueline Cvinar, a professor at the University of Massachusetts Lowell, conducted a literature review with the same inquiry. She wanted to compare suicide bereavement with that in response to natural loss. Her conclusion was that most authors she researched agreed that suicide grief is singular. She discovered a few reasons why. For example, apart from the natural sadness and sense of loss that follow the death of a significant other, those affected by self-inflicted death experience shame, guilt, anger, and social isolation. They fear being misunderstood and find little support from family and friends due to the inherent stigma associated with suicide.

It is common for survivors to ask themselves, "How did I not see it coming?" This adds a heavy burden to all affected, which may be aggravated by family dysfunction and the sense of having been rejected by the deceased. Shame and guilt contribute to not being able to move forward. Before I zoom in on the aspects inherent to suicide, I need to be clear that by no means do I want to imply that this type of mourning is more painful than others. A loss is a loss; pain is pain—we all experience death differently. More than anything, I want to honor this reality, but it is important for us counselors to be aware that there are certain aspects of grief that should not be ignored when suicide is on the table. In that regard, this chapter can be seen as a guide; my aim is to cover these themes objectively, illustrated by anecdotes of real-life stories from the families I interviewed.

As counselors, we should try to keep some of these unique elements of suicide grief in the back of our minds because, many times, our patients will not feel comfortable bringing them up. As we know, feelings like shame and guilt can be tracked in silence as much as in words. If we know what survivors go through, we can tune into the unsaid, the non-verbal expressions, the emotions our clients are unprepared or unwilling to share with us. By being aware of these, we can help our patients unlock these unbearable aspects of their grief. We can help them move forward toward more fulfilling lives, integrating their loss with the challenges faced by the new reality that lies ahead.

What makes suicide bereavement unique

The death of a loved one is unquestionably one of the most painful experiences we can have, no matter how they died. A mix of overwhelming emotions will be present, whether it's fear, sadness, shock, numbness, or despair. With suicide, though, the loss will be followed by internal and external reactions that don't usually come with other types of deaths.

Tom Smith, author of *The Unique Grief of Suicide: Questions & Hope*, wrote his book after losing his twenty-six-year-old daughter, Karla. Prior to her death, he had lost both parents, a sister, a brother, and other relatives. Still, he states that Karla's was the hardest to face, not just because she was his daughter—the death of a child is considered the most painful loss there is—but the fact that it was suicide:

"None of the grief following those deaths does to me what Karla's death does. Ongoing suicide grief, though not persistent anymore, is a permanent part of

my emotional DNA. I will die with that loss tattooed on my soul . . . Suicide puts a perspective on life that shrinks the importance of everything except the death."

He discusses some of the reasons why he believes this type of grief is different from others. Voluntary death brings additional complications to one's bereavement. First of all, since suicide is a choice, it adds a sense of abandonment and rejection to those left behind. It is also sudden and violent; but, unlike accidents, where society sees the bereaved as victims, the stigma—real or imagined—and shame associated with suicide will likely isolate the mourner, because no one will know what to say. There is no script for this kind of loss. It also creates a heavy cloud of unanswered questions as well as blame, fear, regrets, and embarrassment for the family.

In *After Suicide: A Ray of Hope for Those Left Behind*, Eleanora Betsy Ross, who lost her husband to suicide and worked with support groups, adds some relevant considerations to those described by Tom Smith. For example, instead of getting community support, the bereaved is usually isolated. Their privacy is not respected, but invaded not only by those around them, but sometimes also due to the death being followed by an investigation. Instead of reassurance, mourners may experience gossip or have their feelings ignored. Words of comfort are substituted by silence, and the focus is not on the family's bereavement, but on the act of suicide itself. The shock response is not tempered, but heightened, and worst of all, families are often pulled apart instead of brought together by the shared loss.

In one powerful sentence, Ross summarizes the impact of suicide on a loved one: "Death is what happened to the person who died; suicide is what is happening to those who are left alive."

William Worden argues that suicide is the most difficult bereavement for a family to face and resolve. One of the reasons for that is the discrepancy in interpretation of the death. As a coping mechanism, individuals may have distorted thinking about it; myths are created. One may accept suicide as the means of death, while others will never come to terms with the reality of it and hold on, for example, to the idea of an accident.

As a result, communication and healing will be harder for all. Worden highlights three themes that are only found in suicide grief: "Why did they do it?", "Why didn't I prevent it?" and "How could they do this to me?" All of these leave the bereaved with a sense of doubt, guilt, and self-loathing, which will have a lasting impact on their grief. The second question was also brought to my attention by Terry Hargrave, PhD and professor of marital and family therapy at Fuller Theological Seminary in Pasadena, California:

> *"It does say something about the one that is left. Not everybody is meaning to send that message, but that's inevitable. The person that's left is going to feel that 'you were saying something about me,' or at the minimum, 'I wasn't important enough for you to make another decision.'"*

In 1972, Dr. Albert Cain published the pioneering book, *Survivors of Suicide*, at a time when the field of suicidology was in its early stages. He was one of the first to closely study survivors, and he identified nine common reactions. The first one is reality distortion, such as denial, repression, contradictory beliefs, lies, and redefinition of reality. The result is families creating myths surrounding the death.

The second, tortured object-relations, can be observed in neediness, destruction of relationships, hunger for/fear of closeness, loneliness, and need to reenact separation.

The third is overwhelming guilt, followed by disturbed self-concept, expressed by shame, dishonor, the stigma of being cast away, abandoned, unwanted, or unlovable. Impotent rage is the fifth. This reaction is a result of an intense sense of rejection fed by social "branding," as well as being perceived as a burden.

The sixth is identification with the deceased/suicide. Depression and self-destructiveness come next and may be bred by shame, guilt, unmet yearning, unresolved grief, self-hatred, 'deadness,' apathy, withdrawal, sadness, and despair.

The eighth reaction is search for meaning. Mourners may repeat and reconstruct events prior to the suicide in a continuous quest for "Why"? The ninth and last common reaction of survivors is incomplete mourning, which may happen due to concealment of the act, as well as a guilt-engendered social avoidance. Both hamper the process of mourning. Those are just some of the aspects observed in suicide grief. Apart from the unique struggles it entails, even the ones that are similar to other kinds of deaths need to be looked at through special lenses. Some of the emotions, for instance, are either heightened or compounded by the additional elements present in cases of suicide.

In *Suicide and Bereavement*, Dr. Edwin Shneidman, who started the field of suicidology in the United States, writes about this:

> *"These emotions are intensified and aggravated, sometimes to unbearable proportions, by the grim additions of shame, guilt, self-blame, and hostility."*

Take anger as an example. When a person loses someone to a disease or accident, they may feel angry at the circumstances of death. In suicide, though, anger is pervasive; it touches everything and everyone. Anger is directed at the death itself, but also at the deceased; sometimes, it targets indiscriminately God, loved ones, friends, family members, institutions, and, quite often, the bereaved themselves.

This pervasive anger was evident when I interviewed Kesia. Her sister was twenty-four years old when she killed herself. She had a long history of bipolar disorder and had been in crisis for years. The family had tried everything and were very present during her many treatments and relapses. At the time, the sister was living with her boyfriend and had attempted suicide three times in the previous few months.

Kesia described to me the day before the death. Her sister was frantically trying to jump in front of passing cars. Someone called the police ,and when they arrived, she started to cry and scream at them, asking the policemen to shoot her. After being taken to the hospital, where she was heavily medicated, she was brought back home.

"That day, she slept on my lap," Kesia recalls. "When she woke up, she was out of control. In an episode of rage, she got up and went to the home she shared with her boyfriend." Kesia was worried and went there later in the day, only to find her sister already dead.

When I asked her what her initial feelings were, she immediately said, "Anger at the hospital, who should not have sent her home, at her boyfriend, and at everyone who made judgmental comments on Facebook—particularly a pastor, who wrote, 'The family didn't see it coming, now it's too late to cry.'"

Anger always needs probing. Tracy Sandor, who specializes in trauma, recommends that therapists try to find what is being covered by this secondary emotion. She points out, "You will usually find deep sadness underneath. It doesn't take long to get to the heart of it—there is often so much shame."

One of the techniques she uses is the empty chair, in which the client is asked to imagine that a chair is the person they lost. Then, she asks them to talk to the deceased with the question: "If they were here, what would you tell them? Tell the person how pissed you are."

According to her, it helps bring the submerged emotions to the surface. Jessica is a good example of this. I talked to her a few months after her mother killed herself at the age of fifty-four. She told me that her mom was a very active and generous person. She participated in several charities in her hometown and was involved with her church community. However, she had experienced significant traumas in her life, including the loss of her husband early in the marriage, when Jessica was only four months old. She had also lost her father at the age of thirteen. The most recent loss had been her thirty-year-long job.

Jessica believes that her mother was having a hard time adjusting to her new life; she was anxious, depressed, and fearful of aging.

"She started crying about her father's death as if it had just happened," she remembers. Jessica's immediate reaction was anger. First, toward her mother:

"I had many opportunities to leave our town, but never left because she always begged me to stay close to her. I adapted my life around her. I was more of a mother to her than the other way around. After doing everything I did for her, she left me."

Her anger didn't end there. God came next; she was furious at Him. Jessica and her mother used to go to church every week, but she stopped going because of the community's reaction to the suicide. Her anger was equally directed at her extended family, because they kept a distance and couldn't accept the idea of suicide. After I talked for over an hour with her, it became clear that underneath her anger was the painful sense of loneliness created by her mother's death.

She told me, "I expected love from my family and those who were close to us, because they knew how tight our relationship was. Everyone sees me as this strong person, so they didn't think I needed support. I'm still working through my feelings of abandonment."

Disappointment was also present. She felt judged by others. When she decided to continue living in the same home where her mother had taken her life, she heard things like, "Are you crazy? How can you stay there?" and "Didn't you notice that she was sick?"

People would ask her, "Your mother had everything, how could she have done that?" Many tried to give her advice, such as, "Now that your mother is dead, you should try to find a boyfriend."

The ever-present stigma

Stigma is a concept that comes practically blended with the act of suicide; its repercussions cripple the survivor's healing journey in many direct and indirect ways. Stigma generates a wide ripple effect, causing family and friends of the deceased to get entangled in a dense web of painful emotions, mental confusion, additional losses, and personal isolation. Stigma is the word all authors use when writing about suicide. There is no controversy here. The World Health Organization recognizes that there are more taboos attached to the discussion of this issue than to any other form of death. Avoidance behavior is pervasive, leaving little room for survivors to verbalize their emotions and talk about the pain they experience.

Silence is frequently the first consequence of stigma. On the day her brother Deyves killed himself, Mayra was coming home from work when she saw police cars and a large number of people surrounding the house where she lived with him and his wife. Deyves was twenty-four years old and had just had a son.

"Before his death," she remembers, "I had a very active life. I worked, did exercise, painted, and socialized. After that, I felt numb and withdrew from practically everything. There were no words of comfort, only condemnation. Some would say he was burning in hell, others would accuse us of being responsible for his death."

When Mayra went back to work, nobody asked her how she was feeling or if she needed any help. She learned to keep her pain inside and started lying to those who didn't know her story. When asked about her family, she would simply say she was an only child. With time, even when a friend tried to get close and talk about her brother's suicide, she would shy away from it. "I learned how to avoid empathy," she said. "It was my way to avoid suffering even more."

Her mother Márcia had been following Deyves closely. She knew he was going through marital and other personal problems. They had a close relationship; he opened up to her. At the time of his death, she had convinced her ex-husband to take her son to see a psychologist due to his drug problems. They worried he had become addicted, but the psychologist told the parents they had nothing to worry about. Her next attempt to help was to take him to church, a suggestion he promptly accepted.

Márcia remembers him crying throughout the service but never going back. The last time she saw him, Márcia tried to calm her son down by affirming that things would get better. He looked at her and whispered, "Sometimes I want to . . .", making the gesture of a knife slashing his own throat. She asked if he was thinking about killing himself, and he replied, "Yes, then I will stop being a problem to everyone."

"Don't be silly. Even if that were true, what is the point if you're dead?" she questioned. Mother and son had a goodbye ritual. Every time they parted, she would say, "Go with God, I love you very much," then he would answer, "Me, too." Both would smile in silence.

On the day of his death, he didn't wait for his mother's goodbye ritual, and before leaving the car, he looked at her and, before she had time to initiate the farewell remarks, he said, "Mom, I love you very much."

Later that day, she heard people say, "Where was this kid's mother? The parents? This only happens to those who don't have God in their hearts."

Márcia has a strong faith and refuses to listen to this kind of judgment. She clung to her religion, which helped her have compassion about Deyves's drastic choice.

It is quite common to hear from mourners that they don't reveal the act to others, either to avoid re-living it or for fear of having to face uncomfortable questions and condemnation. Survivors usually dose out the amount of disclosure they are willing to give. If the immediate or extended family choose to be silent about it, they may search for other sources of comfort, like friends, religious communities, support groups, or therapy. In one way or the other, suicide crawls around the alleys of one's life story—sometimes hidden, sometimes partially revealed.

A good example of how selective survivors can be on the release of information is the case I wrote about at the beginning of this chapter. As I mentioned before, all three of Miguel's daughters and his ex-wife offered to talk to me, because they believe in the value of fighting the stigma associated with suicide. They were gracious and open with me— not one question was left unanswered. It was clear that they wanted their story to make a difference to others, but even with this level of openness, they all revealed their selectiveness when it came to talking about it.

Gabriela told me that sometimes, not only does she hide the fact that her father killed himself, but she makes up different methods of death depending on the circumstances. Her guard comes down only when the person is close to her. That's when she makes sure to explain what actually happened so that they understand the context of his death.

Isabela goes even further. Her grief is so intense that she often tries to convince herself that her father died of cancer. She still fights her own stigma. "I used to believe that only crazy people killed themselves," she reveals. "Maybe I don't talk about it because I feel ashamed. I'm still not over it."

Her other sister Ana Paula also used to think that suicide only happened to the mentally ill, but she decided to see a support group that helped her change her views. One of the biggest challenges for them was to fight their own misconceptions about self-inflicted death. Silence is the beginning of a destructive sequence of cause and effect. When the bereaved refuse to talk about their loss, the discomfort of stepping on eggshells will eventually distance survivors from sources of support; as a consequence, they will feel isolated, alone, which will then serve to widen the gap between them and their surrounding communities.

After the death of his daughter Karla, author Tom Smith felt the heaviness created by silence, which he said was more painful than actually talking about it. In *Silent Grief: Living in the Wake of Suicide*, Christopher Lukas and Henry Seiden recognize that between 1987, when the first edition came out, and 2007, when the second version was published, the theme of suicide had become more prominent, particularly online. However, there is still a long road ahead. They explain:

> *"We continue to believe that suicide has a profound, traumatic effect upon individuals left behind, one that is still not entirely recognized by the medical community or the public. Family members and other loved ones feel isolated by the suicidal act and its aftermath."*

Christopher Lukas knows well the destructive effects of silence. His mother killed herself when he was six years old. He was only told by his father ten years later. His aging aunt and uncle also killed themselves. At the funeral services, not a word about suicide was mentioned. In 1984, his closest childhood friend took his own life, and that was the turning point for him. He needed to understand what had happened to them. In his search for solace and tips on how to grieve, Lukas turned to the literature to no avail. After reviewing over 2,200 works on the subject, he found little material covering suicide survivors, so he decided to write the book with Dr. Henry Seiden, a psychoanalyst from New York.

My personal experience is very similar to Luka's. When I wrote the first edition of this book during 2006 and 2007, I was able to find a considerable amount of information on the internet, as well as books written mainly by American and British authors. In Brazil, however, the context was much different. As a matter of fact, the lack of data and references in the area was one of my main drives to write this book.I knew there were thousands of Brazilians going through the loss of a loved one to suicide, and they had nothing to help them understand it or to relate to people who experienced the same.

A lot has changed since then. Over the years, one of my main targets has been educating the media, because their approach to suicide has historically been either inappropriate or non-existent. I still spend considerable time talking to journalists about the issue, making sure they understand that the media plays a central role in combatting the stigma associated with suicide. In 2016, I created a website so that more people can have access to information.

Today there are additional books—though still not many—about the theme, and the Brazilian media has dramatically improved its coverage of suicide; but, as we know well, changing social values and beliefs takes time. By not being able to share their pain, many still face the heavy burdens of silence, guilt, and fear that come with voluntary death. Another direct consequence of the stigma is shame, which can often come in perfect synchrony with guilt.

Even now, thirty years after the death of her husband, counselor Leslie Storm still feels the effects of the shame. "It took twenty years for my mother to talk about it. I became estranged from her for a year because of a remark she made. My sister told her kids that he had died in a fishing accident; my friends couldn't deal with the shame of it all, and my father never mentioned the suicide."

I have never talked to a suicide survivor who didn't experience some degree of guilt. It is probably the most universal emotion when it comes to self-inflicted death. Most of the time, this self-consuming feeling derives from questions such as, "Could I have done something to prevent it?", "How did I not see it?", and most prevalent of all, the infinite versions of "What if?"

Guilt doesn't have to be directly related to the death itself; it shows up in many different ways and at different levels of intensity. For seven years, Georgena Eggleston was stuck in her guilt for not holding her son's hand minutes before his death. Maybe she could have stopped what happened next, she thought. Reed, her son, was the epitome of an aspiring teenager: popular, good-looking, a straight-A student, an athlete. Failing was not part of his life, but one day, after drinking with friends, he was caught in a breath test and was suspended from school for three days and banned from the basketball team for the rest of that season.

For him, the shame was unbearable. In an act of impulse, while Georgena was comforting his girlfriend, he went home and shot himself. In her book, *A New Mourning: Discovering the Gifts in Grief*, she writes, "There was no room in his mind for self-compassion. No mercy could be shown to himself. His rage flipped the switch, and my beloved son was gone."

When I interviewed her, she mentioned how hard it was to forgive herself for not taking his hand before he went home. "I was stuck with grief for seven years. For seven years, I blamed myself for his death," she said.

In the story of Gabriela and her sisters, they all gave love and assistance to their father Miguel. They were present, took him to the doctor, brought him to stay with them, and talked on a daily basis, but that was not sufficient to stop them from feeling guilt. The last weeks of his life, Miguel was at Gabriela's home in Florida. After replaying every single day they spent together in her mind, what stood out to her was the moment she dropped him off at the airport. "I didn't accompany him. I could have stayed with him for another hour," she sighed.

Isabela was coming to see him the following day. They talked on the phone and she felt that he was aloof, acting strange and out of character. Before he hung up, he told her, "I love you."

Later on the same day, she was with friends at a happy hour, and couldn't get those words out of her head. Isabela started feeling sick and went home. That night, she couldn't sleep well. The following day, she woke up to the news of her father's suicide. For her, that was the frozen moment that guilt wouldn't let her forget. "I could have talked to him more deeply; I could have asked him what he was feeling," she told me. Her words took me back to what my sister felt the last day she saw my father. Renata could sense that there was something wrong and that he was in pain, and for years she blamed herself for not asking what was happening.

In the book *Working With the Dying and Bereaved*, Pauline Sutcliffe, Guinevere Tufnell, and Ursula Cornish acknowledge how stigma impacts the bereaved. They contend the "social stigma of suicide contributes to family shame and cover-up of the circumstances. Secrecy distorts communication and isolates families from social support."

William Worden adds that when feeling guilty, survivors may develop the need to be punished. Through delinquency, self-destruction, and the use of chemical substances, they act out so society will punish them.

Blame can be another face of guilt; they are two sides of the same coin. When guilt is present, pointing a finger works as a way of shifting self-blame. This form of emotional disguise should be closely examined by therapists. Scapegoating may very well be a way of affirming control over the death of a loved one or an attempt to cover one's own guilt. There is always someone or something to blame: the doctor, a new wife or husband, a demanding job, a neglectful parent, a disease, or the person who ended their life. I often hear the phrase, "I know that no one is responsible for their death, but . . ." followed by the blaming of oneself, others, or both. Even when the loved one leaves a note saying there was no one to blame for their decision, words are insufficient to eliminate blame and guilt.

Ivo told me the story of his daughter Eriele, who was eighteen when she took her own life. On the day of her death, they had lunch. There were no signs, no previous history of mental illness, no problems that he knew of. During their chat, they talked about her professional future. Eriele wanted to be a lawyer just like her dad and was already studying for the exams. She seemed fine and even asked him about the plans for the weekend.

The parents shared custody of their kids, and the following weekend they would be with him. Eriele wanted to eat a piece of pie, so he said he would get it and bring it to her later that day, when they were supposed to meet again. When he dropped her off, nothing unusual happened. They said goodbye, and he drove off.

They were supposed to meet again at 4:30 p.m., but she got home two hours later at 6:40. At 6:50, he arrived to pick her up, but she was dead;

her body had been found by her sister. Eriele had left a note saying that it was no one's fault; she just couldn't take it anymore. "Dead people don't disappoint anyone," she wrote.

Her words were not enough to stop the blaming. "I felt responsible for not noticing that there was something wrong. I feel an unbearable pain, a sense of guilt, impotence, responsibility, and incompetence," he said. His ex-wife and his other kids also blamed him. They would repeat over and over, "You were the last one to be with her. What did you tell her? How could you not have seen it?"

Blaming the deceased is also common and may come in many forms. It can be a maneuver to avoid one's own guilt and emotions that are hard to process. In cases of a long history of mental illness, caregivers may feel angry and devalued, their dedication ignored. They feel betrayed and often name the person's action as a demonstration of cowardice, lack of appreciation, and disregard for other people's feelings. Beneath this narrative, as a therapist, you may discover an underlying sense of failure, particularly in the case of parents who lose a child.

The expressed anger may also represent a displacement of unresolved conflicts with the deceased. This is compounded by the reality that there is no more time to repair the relationship. One of the ways to disguise this painful awareness that there will be no future chance to rebuild connection is to idealize the dead. In her book, *Necessary Losses*, Judith Viorst writes:

> *"Idealization allows us to keep our thoughts pure and to keep guilt at bay. It is also a way of repaying the dead, of making restitution, for all the bad we have done — or imagined we've done — to them."*

Suicide within the family context

We have a cultural tendency to look at suicide as an isolated manifestation of a troubled individual. After hearing about a new case, the immediate question asked is "What happened?" as if one single occurrence could generate an act of this magnitude. However, this is rarely applicable. There may be a significant factor involved, maybe a major trigger, but the act is often just the tip of the iceberg, especially when we examine it within the family context. Not that we should investigate the matter with fingers pointed at family members. On the contrary, our aim should always be to help loved ones identify sensitive hurdles that may need to be worked through so that grief can be processed and relationships improved.

I remember thinking about the relationship between suicide and family dynamics when I met Pattie in a café in Portland, Oregon. I had never met her before, but as soon as she heard through a mutual friend that I was writing about survivors, she volunteered to talk. She had a sweet and fragile smile. Like me, Pattie had also lost a father who had been an alcoholic, but that was where our family similarities ended. Fortunately, in mine, we tended to express our feelings and, no matter how bad the situation, we were hardly kept in the dark. With her, it was the opposite—secrets, anger, and cover-ups were the norm.

When her parents got married, her father was a strong, handsome man, an athlete who worked as a petroleum engineer. He volunteered for the Navy and stayed in New Guinea for a while, where, Pattie believes, he had a hard time. After that, he took a job in Iran. However, following a big fire in the oil well he was responsible for, her father got fired. The shame he felt was overwhelming. From that point on, things were never the same. He started drinking, the marriage began to crumble, and the family dynamics reflected just that. They lived in silence about the troubles at home; nothing was discussed, so emotions kept bubbling up until they burst.

Pattie is the middle child and had two sisters. In her early teens, the youngest started using drugs and alcohol and partied non-stop. At sixteen, she ran away for a few days. Her father was angry but asked Pattie to deal with it and talk to her sister. She recalled that conversation: "I took her to the beach, and she said, 'You are the only one I love.'"

Pattie still feels responsible for her little sister, and they remain very close to this day. "If we didn't have each other, we would have been lost," she told me. The oldest was estranged from the family and, according to Pattie, she used to be angry at everyone. She left home at the age of twenty-one, before their father's suicide.

The girls had no male role model. After returning from war, their father was a different man. She remembers one day, he broke down drunk and cried, repeating, "All those boys killed, all those boys killed."

The day before his death, he came to the house to see his kids, but by then his ex-wife had a restraining order against him, so he wasn't allowed in. Pattie told me this with teary eyes, and added: "I've never known why she did that." This is one of the unanswered questions she carries to this day.

On the following day, he called his ex-wife to say two things: that he loved her and that he was going to kill himself. One day later, she got a call from the motel where he was staying, asking her to come in. Pattie recalls the moment her mother told her the news. "I remember feeling relief, because there was so much fear around us. It took me years to understand what I really felt that day."

Her mother worked hard to hide the suicide. She told friends and the girls that he had died of a heart attack. The oldest sister repeated this version of the facts until the day she died. It took her mother years to ever mention it to Pattie. "She was too ashamed of it and felt guilty about the effect it had on us." There was a positive shift in their relationship, though. After his death, Pattie's mom became more involved in their lives.

Pattie is now a retired counselor. Her profession helped her understand the hidden pain he was fighting internally. She believes he suffered from untreated Post-Traumatic Stress Disorder (PTSD) which at the time was only beginning to be researched. She also identifies the family patterns and the effect of his death on the whole family. In the past, her younger sister attempted suicide, and so did she. "I have been through the trauma; I know how it goes on and on. There was a part of me that believed he loved me, but you feel you were not enough. I wish I could have said, 'We love you for who you are, please don't do that,'" she uttered.

Pattie believes that what helped her heal and rebuild her life was therapy, art, and love. She feels heard and loved by her husband. She also regrets the suicide attempt and says she wouldn't do it again because of the pain it would inflict on her sister. During therapy, her psychoanalyst guided her through her past so that she could bring to the surface layers of suppressed guilt and shame built over the years. By creating beautiful, delicate art—she is a painter and a poet—Pattie gives language to her pain. She was generous enough to authorize me to share one of her poems with my readers.

Like Father Like Daughter

Somewhere within me a river
heavy with black water surges,
hurtles my dead father head first,
the whites of his eyes glinting.

No, it was not the drink that killed him.
Yes he drank whiskey – gallons,
not enough to finish him off,

sufficient to shred his liver, black-out
his heart, gut his insides.
It was the white pills he swallowed –
all of them, a thousand of them,
and now he swims white in the dark river,
cries for me to get him out
or get in with him.

What happened to Pattie can be observed in many families touched by
suicide. There are two aspects I want to emphasize: voluntary death may
be the tipping point of an already-complicated, long-term situation; and,
when it does happen, it is crucial that we investigate its effects, because
the way family members historically deal with pain and loss will likely
be exacerbated. In the following paragraphs, I will compile what several
authors have learned through their experience with grieving families.
Some are not specifically about suicide, but should nevertheless be
considered during therapy.

William Worden proposes a few interventions with suicide survivors:
reality-test guilt and shame when they are present. Is shame expressed
by scapegoating, for example? Correct denial and distortions by helping
clients face the reality of the loss. Say 'killed himself,' for instance.
It is also important to redefine the image of the deceased, which
may be unrealistic. Work with anger by allowing them to express and
acknowledge it. The sense of abandonment should also be reality-tested;
assess the level of it. Help them find meaning. "Survivors feel the need
to explain death to others, to make sense of it," he points out.

Since Worden mentions denial, I feel compelled to add some
considerations about it. In *Ambiguous Loss: Learning to Live with Unresolved
Grief,* Pauline Boss looks at denial in two ways. On one hand, it can
serve a healthy purpose, providing temporary respite from the harsh
psychological reality of a loss, and therefore reducing stress. On the

other hand, she alerts us about its permissive, long-lasting effect, because it may prevent transformation that would allow moving forward. It invalidates the presence of someone who is still there and causes more distress in families, because each member will be alone in their interpretation and pain. In the end, she says, "Denial is neither something to avoid nor something to advocate. It's a complex response that can be both functional and dysfunctional."

Her approach to denial is in the context of ambiguous losses, which refers to losses that have no closure or understanding. They leave the bereaved with a series of unanswered questions regarding the death of a loved one. The author's remarks made me reflect on suicide and ambiguity. She grew up in an immigrant community in Southern Wisconsin. They had moved there in the early 1900s, leaving family behind in Switzerland. Her father would receive letters from his brother and mother, wondering if they would ever see each other again. "Longing for faraway family members was commonplace," she recalls. Their loss was constant. Even when they were still alive, they were nevertheless absent, and those who had left Switzerland couldn't go back due to poverty and war.

There are two types of ambiguous loss: when the person is physically present but psychologically absent, or not there physically, but remains present psychologically. What characterizes ambiguous loss is uncertainty: the inability to understand what happened. It's the same case with parents whose kids disappear, never to be heard from again, or a soldier who goes to war and doesn't come back, but doesn't have their death officially recognized.

Alzheimer's is another example of someone who remains with you but slowly drifts away. "It is the most devastating because it is unclear, indeterminate . . . a loss that defies closure." Boss adds that it blocks grieving, because hope remains alive. It baffles and it immobilizes the individual who can't make sense of it and doesn't have answers. The uncertainty prevents adjustments—there is little validation for what they feel, and people avoid giving support. The experience exhausts victims, and it freezes families in place.

Unlike other types of death, suicide in many circumstances bears a close resemblance to what is defined as ambiguous loss. Two reasons come to mind: sometimes, there is real doubt about the death itself. Was it really suicide? The second has to do with the ever-present question, "Why?" Even when survivors know it was a voluntary death, many questions remain unanswered. "Why?" haunts them for the rest of their lives. As Dr. Shneidman says, in *Suicide and Bereavement*, "The suicidal person places his psychological skeleton in the survivor's closet."

As survivors, we search for answers, but even when we find them, they are hardly sufficient to answer the fundamental "Why" question; suicide is, at its core, incomprehensible. I witnessed that repeatedly during the interviews with survivors. After hearing their stories, the last question I asked every single one was, "Today, knowing what you know, could you say why they killed themself?" Even the ones who had a very detailed understanding of the circumstances of death—personal crisis, previous losses, mental illness—would stop, think for a while, and have a hard time answering. Most of them said, "No."

Pauline Boss gives tips to therapists when treating ambiguous loss. I will reproduce some of them, because I believe they can be applied to suicide grief as well:

- Consider the fact that this type of loss may never allow people to achieve the detachment that is necessary for closure. Family members may withdraw from one another. As she argues, "The family becomes a system with nobody in it."

- Try to assess the client's tolerance for the unknown, how they deal with feelings. Are they free to express them? Bring the hidden emotions to the table. Help them recognize and name them.
- Consider social aspects because sometimes it is the situation that is sick, not the family, and they may simply have been adapting in dysfunctional ways.
- Encourage them to contact people in similar situations (I will talk about support groups later in this chapter).

Finally, she says, "Ambiguous loss makes us feel incompetent. It erodes our sense of mastery and destroys our belief in the world as a fair, orderly, and manageable place." These are all valuable things to consider when treating clients and families who experience this kind of loss, because these individuals will come in with little validation of their pain.

Complicated grief

Trying to define complicated grief is no easy task because, as we've discussed before, grieving follows no checklist. On the other hand, this issue is of central importance when treating survivors, because they have a higher incidence of traumatic or complicated grief and PTSD. In an article published in the British Journal of Psychiatry, Dr. Holly defines complicated grief as "intrusive symptoms of yearning, longing for and searching for the deceased, as well as four or more persistent symptoms of trauma as a result of the death."

Some of these symptoms are avoidance of reminders of the deceased, purposelessness, feelings of futility and that life is meaningless, numbness, detachment, shock, excessive death-related bitterness, and identification with harmful behaviors resembling those suffered by their descendant. According to William Worden in *Grief Counseling and Grief Therapy*, some

216

factors may lead to complicated reactions. The first one has to do with the relationship with the deceased. Did it have unexpressed hostility and ambivalence? If so, anger and guilt may be highly present.

Another example is when the person who died was an extension of the person left behind, so the client may resist the loss, because it means losing part of their own self. Death may also open old wounds, which is the case with an abusive relationship. This can provoke extreme reactions, because it reminds the bereaved of something they wished for but never had.

I would add that it is like placing a period at the end of a sentence. It becomes final. The person is gone, so the chances for rebuilding the lost relationship are gone for good. This concept reminds me of what Kübler-Ross says in *The Tunnel and the Light*: "The greatest grief you can ever experience . . . is the grief over love that you have never experienced."

Worden invites us to dig into the patient's history in terms of how they have reacted to past losses. If they have a pattern of extreme reactions, there are higher chances of repeating them. Personality is also key. Do they have a high tolerance for stress? What is their self-concept?

The circumstances of death play a part as well. Ambiguous and concurrent deaths may lead to complicated grief. Finally, there are social factors: how is the death seen in their social environment? Is it accepted or negated? Do communities give support to the bereaved? These are some of the considerations he highlights.

Worden offers us additional clues that may point toward complicated grief, with the caveat that these are by no means determinants in and of themselves:

- A person speaks of the dead with intense fresh pain, regardless of the timeframe of death.

- Minor events trigger intense reaction.
- Development of physical symptoms like those the deceased experienced before death (these may recur annually).
- Compulsion to imitate the dead person, which is a way to compensate the loss by identifying with it.
- Self-destructive impulses, phobia, inability to move material possessions belong to the deceased, the development of illnesses related to death, and history of subclinical depression.

In *The Worst Loss: How Families Heal from the Death of a Child*, child therapist Barbara Rosof talks about stressors that interfere with grief: previous history of significant losses, severe stress in the current life, drugs, and alcohol, and negative or unsupportive responses from others. She defines suicide as "the worst failure" for parents because of the personal rejection they feel, the stigma, and the "cloud of fear, disapproval, and humiliation" it creates.

Rosof mentions another stressor: the presence of a replacement child, when a child is conceived to take the place of the one who has died, or even a sibling who takes over the role of the lost one. "A replacement child is an act of desperation. Not only does the strategy fail," she explains, "but parents who create a replacement child compound their loss."

One of the most intriguing stories I came upon during the interviews for this book was of Andrea, a woman in her thirties who not only took the place of her dead sister Adriana, but had her name changed by family members. Although this was not legally done, she was never called by the name that was assigned to her at birth, and the psychological impact of being called by her sister's name was disastrous to the building of her identity.

In Dying to Be Free: *A Healing Guide for Families After a Suicide*, Beverly Cobain and Jean Larch address the factors that may compound one's grief. Beverly's own story is a moving one. Her account comes not only from working as a psychiatric nurse but also from her personal life. She experienced three family suicides, including her cousin Kurt Cobain, the lead musician from the band Nirvana.

The authors refer to the double rejection felt by survivors: by the person who took their life and by society. A closed casket may also compound grief, because it makes it harder to accept the reality of death. In cases when families had no prior knowledge of the suffering of the deceased, it may raise the question of "really knowing" the person, which adds pain to mourning.

Another factor Cobain and Larch site is the lack of freedom to grieve for as long as they need. People expect the bereaved to move on according to their views on the "right" timing of grief. In a delicate passage from Notes for the Everlost: A Field Guide to Grief, author Kate Inglis touches on this:

> *"You are exactly where you need to be. Fiercely protect your grieving ground . . . your sacred lifelong dialogue with death is yours distinctively. We are all having the same dialogue in parallel, but it is to each their own. Your relationship with death is yours to forward, grow into and bargain with."*

When writing her memoir, *The Long Goodbye*, Meghan O'Rourke discussed how social expectation and pressure may actually represent a deeper fear. About losing her mother to cancer in 2008, she says:

> *"I felt that the world expected me to absorb the loss and move forward, like some kind of emotional warrior. One night I heard a character on 24h (a TV sitcom) – the president of the United States – announce that grief was a 'luxury' she couldn't 'afford right now.'*

> *This model represents an old American ethic of muscling through pain by*

throwing yourself into work; embedded in it is a desire to avoid looking at death."

O'Rourke reminded me of an underlying aspect that frequently surrounds grief: fear of death. It should never be taken for granted when treating the bereaved, particularly in suicide, because if the client is a member of the family, chances are they will think about what that represents in terms of biological inheritance. After the death of a significant other, survivors become apprehensive about themselves and their siblings.

When I was researching for this book, many survivors would mention that they were afraid of killing themselves. There was a great sense of anxiety regarding hereditary traits. To some, this served as a warning sign for self-care, but to others, it brought an eerie sense of hopelessness and future doom. I heard statements like, "I will not end up like him," or "I also have depression, does that mean I will also kill myself?"

Death anxiety hovers widely over grief. Psychoanalyst and prolific author Irvin Yalom explores this theme in *Staring at the Sun: Overcoming the Terror of Death:*

> *"For some of us the fear of death manifests only indirectly, either as generalized unrest or masqueraded as another psychological symptom; other individuals experience an explicit and conscious stream of anxiety about death, and for some of us the fear of death erupts into terror that negates all happiness and fulfillment."*

He reminds us therapists that although death is a difficult subject to bring up, it should not be avoided:

> *"Death . . . is always with us, scratching at some inner door, whirring softly, barely audibly, just under the membrane of consciousness. Hidden and disguised, leaking out in a variety of symptoms, it is the wellspring of many of our worries, stresses, and conflicts."*

How families are impacted

The trauma experienced by survivors is of a long-term nature and should be regarded and treated as such. Suicide leaves many questions unanswered. It is a poignant reminder of unfinished business, of words unspoken and with no second chances to speak them. When it comes to the impact of suicide on families, two additional aspects should be considered. Apart from the already-mentioned dread of genetics, the act sends out significant meanings to those left behind, particularly when they are children and look up to their parents as role models.

Roberta's (pseudonym) story exemplifies this. Her father had always been an unpredictable man. As a child, she remembers him as being emotionally unstable. He had several affairs and a belligerent relationship with her mother. Sometimes he would scream and break objects around the house. During his fits of rage, her mother would tell her to pretend to be sleeping.

They also had serious financial difficulties. Roberta told me, "I would go to school so that I could eat. My mom would bring food from work." On top of that, her sister had serious recurrent health problems, so there was little time for Roberta.

At the age of ten, Roberta went through two deeply traumatic experiences. One day, her wailing father placed her on his lap, tightened a rope around her neck, and tried to kill her. During the ordeal, she remembers following her mom's advice and pretending to be asleep. In that same week, he killed himself in front of her with the same rope. She recalls looking at him, unable to move. Then, she turned around and left. For ten years, Roberta couldn't remember what had happened to her father or even what his name was. This reaction is congruent with what we know of traumatic memories. They are often suppressed.

In *Death and Trauma: The Traumatology of Grieving*, Charles Figley, Brian Bride, and Nicholas Mazza remind us that part of grief therapy is related to reconstructing the events of death:

> *"Normal grief resolution may be impeded without first attending to the traumatic nature of death . . . Remembering the deceased is part of the course of adaptation, reorganization, and recovery . . . In a traumatic memory, it may be overwhelming, making it hard to integrate them without help. "*

Roberta told me that after her father's suicide, things got better. The family grew closer, and the financial situation improved. "This taught me that suicide was a solution, that it solved problems." As a result, in different moments of her life when things got overwhelming, Roberta attempted suicide herself.

Resilience

Dr. George Bonanno, a leading researcher on bereavement and resilience, states:

> *"People who are overwhelmed by sadness get lost in themselves; they withdraw from the world and become mired in an endless preoccupation, an insatiable desire to have the deceased person back again. When that happens, grief has already begun to take over. "*

In the book *The Other Side of Sadness: What the New Science of Bereavement Tells Us About Life After Loss*, he sheds light on what separates those who become consumed by suffering from those who manage to put their lives together.

His studies show that the vast majority of people are resilient, but that doesn't mean that pain is absent during mourning:

"Resilience doesn't mean, of course, that everyone fully resolves a loss, or finds a state of 'closure.' Even the most resilient seem to hold onto at least a bit of wistful sadness. But we are able to keep on living our lives and loving those still present around us."

What he says may sound quite obvious, but when we think about what brings clients to therapy, a particular section of his statement is of major relevance to therapists: "Even the most resilient seem to hold onto at least a bit of wistful sadness."

One of the questions I asked the counselors I interviewed was what brought their patients in. Practically all of them mentioned, in one form or another, the unrealistic expectation of being free of pain: a natural, albeit utterly unachievable, human response.

Bonanno makes another crucial point about resilience. The literature on bereavement is profuse in cataloging the negative symptoms of grief, but not much attention is given to the flip side. Worse yet, mourners who experience joy even in the early days of loss are often "dismissed as examples of avoidance or denial," he says. As a clinical psychologist, he refutes this notion, but not in an antagonistic tone—quite the contrary. With balance and empirical data, Bonanno elucidates both the devastating effects of grief and our prevalent human capacity for moving beyond it.

One of the themes explored by Bonanno is the interrelation between the memory of the deceased and the processing of grief. He explains:

"People who are able to deal with a loved one's death, and who are able to accept the finality of the loss, are also able to find comfort in memories of that person the relationship is not completely gone . . .

. . . those who are more debilitated by loss, find it harder to hold onto positive memories, as if they can no longer find the person they lost, as if the memories are hidden from them. The pain of grief, it seems, can block all memories of the good."

He argues that traditional theories of grief portray resilience as an illusion. His research findings point in the opposite direction:

"Resilient people are actually less likely than others to use avoidance and distraction as coping strategies. They are less inclined to evade thinking about the loss, or to deliberately occupy their minds to avoid confronting the pain."

When I read his observations regarding the difficulty some find holding onto positive memories, I immediately associated it with a unique aspect of suicide grief: the image of the final act itself. I have often heard from family members—particularly those who find the body—that this single moment overrides most of the previous memories they have of the deceased. If a prolonged mental illness has also been present, behavioral and psychological symptoms may have the same effect. The lively father who developed depression in the last months of his life, for example, becomes just that, as if years of his healthy self were erased by the onset of a disease.

This aspect of grief should be part of the reality check of therapy, because by expanding a client's perception of the relationship, therapists can help them get unstuck. It can equally help dissolve some of the guilt they often feel for "not doing enough." Frequently, when examining the patient's relationship history, you will find that they actually did their best. Tamara Webb, who works as a therapist in Portland, Oregon, told me the story of a patient who came to her due to unrelenting grief after the suicide of her daughter, who had jumped off a bridge. The mother was stuck on the young woman's last hours, as well as the imaginary moment of her jump. The client's mental state and inability to break the barrier of time made it hard to work through her grief. "It was so overwhelming," Webb observed, "that expanding the dialogue was really hard."

For therapists, the study of resilience is paramount, because although there are some people who are naturally more resilient than others, if counselors understand specific coping mechanisms and traits that help soothe the healing process, they can guide clients toward those paths.

Bonanno lays out positive factors that are present in individuals who cope well: physical health, a broader network of friends and family, fewer life stressors, higher levels of education, and better financial resources. Psychological characteristics such as flexibility, confidence, and optimism are also emphasized. As a counselor, it may not be possible to alter a patient's view on life, but it is possible to foster significant changes, such as the broadening of their social support and the adopting of a healthier lifestyle.

Another point Bonanno makes directly related to therapy is the finding that resilience is closely associated with what he calls, "a broader repertoire of behaviors." He mentions the flexibility to express or suppress emotions as an example of this repertoire. Depending on the circumstances, the ability to adjust to particular situations is necessary for one's self-protection. Therapists can help clients find the middle ground. At times, patients may be so debilitated that expressing pain is impossible; or the opposite, they may be so focused on the loss that it is all they talk about with just about anyone, including strangers. As a result, people pull away from them.

Bonanno makes a distinction between grief and depression; other clinicians do the same, so I will comprise what I have learned with my research, citing the original sources so that you can go back to them for further investigation. They should not be taken as diagnostic tools nor considered absolute, but these observations serve as an initial reference to understand where your patient is in their grief. The author pinpoints one central distinction between the two:

> *"The symptoms of depression have no object. They are global and undifferentiated and include such difficulties as a feeling of worthlessness, fatigue, the inability to concentrate, diminished interest or pleasure in activities that would normally be rewarding, reduced or exaggerated appetite, and difficulty maintaining normal sleep patterns. The yearning of prolonged grief, by contrast, is entirely focused on one thing: finding the lost loved one."*

In *Getting Grief Right*, Dr. Patrick O'Malley and Tim Madigan point out that in grief, the bereaved are more likely to seek help and connection. In clinical depression, isolation is the most common endpoint. Feelings such as sadness and anger are magnified in grief; when depressed, feelings are generally numbed. Although painful, mourning is life- and soul-affirming, while in depression, self-loathing and a sense of personal insignificance are present.

William Worden also differentiates these two states. According to him, in grief, there is usually no loss of self-esteem. Guilt is associated with specific aspects of the death, the world feels poor and empty, and negative evaluations of the world and expectations of the future are transient. In depression, self-esteem is lost, there is a general sense of culpability, the person feels poor and empty, and the individual's unfavorable view of self, world and future are long-lasting.

One of the most compelling accounts of depression I have read is *Darkness Visible: A Memoir of Madness*, written by the American novelist William Styron, author of *Sophie's Choice* and other prized books. His memoir was first published in 1989 in the magazine Vanity Fair and later expanded into a book. Styron knew nothing about the disease when it struck him, and it took him months of unhelpful treatments to finally ask his own family for him to be hospitalized, when suicidal ideation took over his thoughts and emotions. He writes:

"With their minds turned agonizingly inward, people with depression are usually dangerous only to themselves. The madness of depression is, generally speaking, the antithesis of violence. It is a storm indeed, but a storm of murk.

Many of the artifacts of my house had become potential devices for my own destruction: the attic rafters (and an outside maple or two) a means to hang myself, the garage a place to inhale carbon monoxide, the bathtub a vessel to receive the flow from my opened arteries. The kitchen knives in their drawers had but one purpose for me."

Styron's memoir is relevant to this discussion not only because of its illuminating depiction of depression, but maybe more importantly, due to his final conviction that the disease had been largely fueled by the unresolved grief of his mother that he only became aware of during his hospitalization. He explains:

"The genetic roots of depression seem now to be beyond controversy, but I'm persuaded that an even more significant factor was the death of my mother when I was thirteen. This disorder and early sorrow, the death or disappearance of a parent, especially a mother before or during puberty appears repeatedly in the literature on depression as a trauma sometimes likely to create nearly irreparable emotional havoc. The danger is especially apparent if the young person is affected by what has been termed 'incomplete mourning' — has, in effect, been unable to achieve the catharsis of grief, and so carries within himself through later years an insufferable burden of which rage and guilt, and not only dammed-up sorrow, are a part, and become the potential seeds of self-destruction."

The writer's words serve to emphasize, once again, the importance of looking at a patient's family grieving patterns, because they may pave the way for future behavior. We can help clients by investigating unprocessed losses with a focus on examining how family members mourned, reacted, and expressed their emotions. In *Recovering from the Losses of Life*, bestselling author and trauma specialist H. Norman Wright gives us insight on the weight brought on by adults when, as children, they were not given the space and freedom to grieve:

> *"The losses of our adult life may be compounded by the remaining unresolved losses of our childhood. We bring these into our adult life like unwelcome excess baggage."*

Actress Mariel Hemingway spent all her life hearing people tell her about the "Hemingway curse," the well-publicized destructive patterns of her ancestors, most notably the suicide of her grandfather, Ernest Hemingway, who shot himself in 1959. In her memoir, *Out Came the Sun: Overcoming the Legacy of Mental Illness, Addiction, and Suicide in My Family*, she walks us through her memories as a way of opening the window of her own life:

> *"A family is a cracked mirror that nevertheless reflects us accurately. At long last, I am longing to look in that mirror. My family made me and through an act of memory, I can now remake it.*

> *For years, I pushed aside the most painful and difficult aspects of my family history or buried them deep inside so that I could move forward with everyday tasks. I am done pushing things aside. Instead, I have decided to look at my life directly, to be clear-eyed about its sorrows but also its joys. This book not only gives me voice – it is my voice."*

Our bodies as conduits of pain

Dr. Bessel van der Kolk is one of the world's leading experts on PTSD. His book, *The Body Keeps the Score: Brain, Mind, and Body in the Healing of Trauma*, is a must-read for any therapist who wants to understand how trauma leaves its imprint on an individual's body. Frequently, clients end up in a counselor's office after a long medical investigation that has been unable to diagnose a "proper" illness. Either that, or they have been referred by a doctor who believes psychological treatment is also necessary. In grief, it is no surprise that this is particularly common. Science has produced enough evidence regarding the physical and psychological health risks caused by traumatic experiences, as Van der Kolk explains:

"The emotions and physical sensations that were imprinted during the trauma are experienced not as memories but as disruptive physical reactions in the present.

Being traumatized means continuing to organize your life as if the trauma were still going on — unchanged and immutable — as every new encounter or event is contaminated by the past."

By asking a simple question, he directs us toward one of the paths to achieve healing:

How many mental health problems, from drug addiction to self-injurious behavior, start as attempts to cope with the unbearable physical pain of our emotions? The solution requires finding ways to help people alter the inner sensory landscape of their bodies.

The physical and emotional side effects one experiences after being impacted by suicide will depend on many factors. Closeness to the diseased is a main conduit to more long-lasting suffering; this is why family members require special attention. Van der Kolk argues that memory loss is a common expression of trauma; the events will usually be remembered not as a linear sequence, but rather fragments of images and sensations.

I felt it myself. Years after my father's suicide, I could not even remember if I had been to his funeral, a gap that intrigued and scared me for a long time. Everything that happened the days before and after his death exists in scattered bits and pieces in my mind, and no matter how much effort I put into it, I still cannot make a coherent description of those moments. While writing this book, the only way I could build a narrative close enough to reality was by interviewing friends and family members.

One of the most dramatic accounts I have ever witnessed of the physical and psychological impacts of suicide on a family member was shared with me during the approximately one-and-a half-years when I was contacted by Edgard, a man who had lost his son months before he sent me the first email. As it often happens, he had found my website when researching the subject in Brazil, and then reached me through social media in the hope of sharing his story. We talked and exchanged messages many times, including the day I interviewed him for this chapter.

For one-and-a-half hours, I listened to his unrelenting pain, which had taken an extreme toll on his mind, body, and soul. Edgar was consumed by guilt. His son's suicide had become the center of his life, his marriage was crumbling, and his relationships were destroyed. He had been on medical leave for six months and was taking six different types of psychotropic drugs, including antidepressants, mood stabilizers, and antipsychotic medication. His health was clearly deteriorating.

As a child and young adult, Edgar had experienced an unfathomable sequence of losses. His father had been murdered when he was fourteen years old; at seventeen, he'd lost his mother. Later on, one of his brothers died as a consequence of alcoholism. Edgar had a close relationship with his son, but, after a hostile divorce resulting in Edgar moving to another city, they saw each other very little. His teenage son kept asking him to come back home and, when that didn't happen, they became estranged.

Edgar would constantly drive to see his son, who refused to open the door for him. After years of isolation, drugs, and alcohol, his son killed himself at the age of twenty-two. The young man took his life by ingesting a mixture of vodka and a poison commonly used in Brazil to kill rats. He was rushed to the hospital and seemed to be recovering. On the second day, he said to family members how sorry he was and asked them for forgiveness. After six days, his body gave out, but Edgar was only informed about what had happened when the boy was already gone. He had no chance to say goodbye. "That hurt me so much," Edgar said. "I keep thinking that I could have done something. There is an endless sense of impotence inside of me."

Edgar felt blamed by the rest of the family. He was told that it was his fault, that maybe if he hadn't separated, it wouldn't have happened. Although he feels he tried several times to regain his son's love and presence, nothing erases his mounting guilt. "Why didn't I try harder?" he told me. "Why didn't I forgive him, why didn't I hug him more? I could have been closer to him. I also blame my history. I had no father figure, I didn't know how to be a father. I lived on the streets for a while. These memories and questions haunt my mind."

Although the death of his son had been fairly recent—the interview was conducted a little over a year after the suicide—Edgar seemed to be heading toward a long, tortuous grieving process. He was being treated for both depression and a recently diagnosed schizophrenia. The voices he was hearing repeatedly told him to kill himself, and he had almost done it twice by the time we last talked. Once, he went to his brother's house, where he knew he would find a gun. He got as far as to point it to his own head, but never pulled the trigger. What saved him the second time was a second voice, that of his therapist, who is one of the best examples I've witnessed of compassion and empathy.

His second attempt led him to the top of a building. When looking down, Edgar heard two voices. The first prompted him to jump, saying, "End it all"; the second whispered kindly, "I will take care of you. You are unique and special."

Edgar told me that his therapist's voice was so "real" that he could even smell her breath. Crying, he followed "her advice" —as he had done a few times before—climbed down the wall, left the building, and collapsed on the street.

He explained to me that two things were keeping him alive: his family— Edgar is remarried and has two teenage daughters—and his therapist. I asked him about the treatment because I wanted to know what she did that was so powerful. The answer once again illustrated what most mental health professionals already know: the most powerful healing tool is the therapeutic relationship. "Every time I tell her I want to kill myself, she says, looking into my eyes, 'As long as you are under my care, you will not take your own life. If you stop coming, I will come after you. I will not lose you, Edgar. I will take care of you.' Her words strengthen me," he said.

Edgar's story is extreme, but many of the professionals I interviewed mentioned the presence of physical health issues in patients with mental health illnesses. This is an important dimension of therapy when it comes to grief. As Alice Miller states in *The Body Never Lies*:

> *"Frequently, physical illnesses are the body's response to permanent disregard of its vital functions. One of our most vital functions is the ability to listen to the true story of our own lives."*

Most training programs in the area give little attention to this aspect of therapy; physical manifestations are mostly included in the content of trauma classes. Finding professionals who could talk to me about the somatization of pain or who used techniques involving the body was not an easy task.

Marika Van Adelsberg was one of them. She follows the Integrative Body Psychotherapy approach (IBP) which focuses on the intimate connection between body, mind, and spirit. She told me of a patient who came in with extreme sadness and breathing difficulties. Marika placed him on a table and guided him through an exercise during which the client rocks his pelvis while performing a specific breathing technique.

After a while, the patient's breathing improved and tears started rolling down his face as talked about his father who had recently died. "When I did something wrong, he used to lock me in a closet," he revealed to Marika. She interpreted what happened: "It was that eight-year-old boy that was so angry at his father for locking him up that he was frozen. He couldn't cry for his death because he was stuck in that anger. So, by just getting in the body, we were able to get there. I worked with the boy who was angry, who never got to tell his daddy 'why did you lock me up?' He never got to address that with his dad, and the anger stayed there his whole life," she explained.

When I came to Georgena Egglestone's office, I knew about the suicide of her son and how the experience had transformed her life, but I had no knowledge about her work. Having been a speech pathologist for many years, she now specializes in trauma and grief as a certified Rubenfels Synergist. This method's main premise is that our memories, thoughts, and emotions are stored in our body; how this connection is expressed affects every aspect of our lives. The aim of the synergist is to listen attentively to the body, allowing the client to identify these relationships, and many times, reconnect what has been severed for most of their lives.

In most interviews, listening to the individual's narrative is enough, but when I talked to therapists who applied some kind of holistic approach, experimenting made a difference. Both Marika and Georgena helped me sample their work by applying some of their techniques on me. Maybe because I am of Latin origins, I feel quite comfortable with the idea of touch and physical proximity. However, in both cases, the hands-on exposure made me more understanding about the common resistance of therapists and patients to break the body barrier, particularly in the United States where boundaries are strongly enforced.

Marika gave me a rope, and we both held on to it while I breathed in a specific manner. While we talked, looking into each other's eyes and never losing track of the breathing, I would pull the rope in my direction. In a soft tone of voice, she would emphasize that we were connected to each other and that she would not let go of the rope. This symbolized our relationship at that moment. For a client, it would be her way of saying, "I will provide a safe place and will be here with you."

Georgena's technique was different. She started by touching my head while letting me know all along what she was going to do and why. When dealing with the body, safety and predictability are paramount because of the way trauma is physically present. Sometimes, touch can trigger painful memories, so informing the patient is a way not only to bring awareness to the here and now, but also to diminish tension. Georgena told me that even though her clients know of her emphasis on working with the body, a few prefer a more traditional therapy. "Some don't get on the table, we just talk," she explains. "For them, I ask about what they are feeling in their body. Then, it's an opportunity to dig into the physical work."

I remember her performing guided imagery while she paid attention to my tightness and temperature. This is one of the ways she helps her patients get in touch with their emotional selves. With a calm and soothing tone, she would ask me to identify where I "felt" the images I visualized, which for me was a beach back in my hometown. "I listen for the metaphors, I'm seeing the images, feeling the state of what is happening with their creating of this," she told me.

At the end of the session, she usually asks, "What is it you're taking with you?" The experience was quite powerful to me, and I left with many reflections in my mind regarding how I store my losses in my own body. Still, the way I described "reflections in my mind" shows how we all need to work to integrate our selves instead of rationalizing feelings and emotions.

Support groups

One of the most helpful forms of healing for survivors is support groups, and I could not end this chapter without talking about their immense value. By being among individuals who have experienced the same type of loss, family members encounter a safe haven for their fears. Fortunately, this type of resource is slowly becoming more accessible. Support groups are places where grievers feel comfortable to cry and express their deeper emotions knowing that, albeit to different degrees, everyone there knows the depths of their pain. Most importantly, they will not be judged or blamed for the death of a loved one. The World Health Organization has a detailed online manual on how to start a group.

The scarcity of this kind of initiative is well-exemplified in Brazil. Psychologist Dr. Karen Scavacini created the first survivor's support group in São Paulo, the largest city in the country, with a population of over twelve million people. And we are not talking about decades ago; this happened very recently, in 2013. On the first day, no one showed up, she told me. Today, she coordinates four groups in the state and one in the city of Rio de Janeiro. She is a rare case—a facilitator who is not a survivor herself.

Karen's groups, and this is common elsewhere, are open to survivors regardless of the timeframe of their loss. Frequently, when members begin to share their stories, they feel relieved and quite surprised by the overall collective reaction. "I hear this a lot: 'So I can really talk?' or 'This is the first time I cried without being interrupted,'" she says. The groups carry stories of suicides as recent as a few weeks to thirty years ago, which just shows how lengthy grief can be, particularly within the silence that surrounds this form of death.

Support groups offer many advantages. They are carried out within a framework of confidentiality. Members have higher levels of empathy, which fosters openness. They feel less judged and isolated, and there is mutual respect. All are encouraged to share, and even their most extreme emotions are not silenced by others. Neither are tears.

Another advantage is how the wide range of stories takes the weight off the member's shoulders. "They see that it can happen to anyone, and for many different reasons. They begin to see that suicide is multidimensional, and they are not alone. There is value in that," says Dr. Luciana Cescon, who facilitates a group in Santos, a city in the metropolitan area of São Paulo.

It is important to note that although most survivors find relief and a sense of community from this kind of environment, support groups are not beneficial for everyone. "Some leave worse than how they came," Cescon warns, "because it depends on their personality traits. Sometimes, when they see members share their pain, it adds to their own, and it is just too much to take in."

For almost a year in 2017, I was a member of a support group. It was an eye-opener for me. Not that I didn't believe in it—not at all—it just hadn't been on my radar. When my father died in 2005, back in Brazil, I had never ever heard of a support group, and I'm pretty sure there were none back then. In my initial meetings, I remember feeling that I had no right to be there. Some had just lost a family member and it was all very raw, so I tended not to talk much. I mostly listened, because I didn't want to "rob" them of their chance to process their grief.

With time, I realized that my experience could have precisely the opposite effect. One day, one of the members approached me and said, "When I hear you talk about your father, it gives me hope, because I know that, with time, I can feel better." Her statement was a turning point for me. From that day on, I became more participative, which also provoked immediate reactions from other members. At the end of a particularly emotional session for me, one of them said: "I often wondered what you were doing here. I'm glad that now you are finally sharing."

Final notes

During the year I researched for this chapter, I found a rich body of work in the theme of grief therapy, but, by the time I finished laying out the main issues I wanted to focus on, I still had relevant material left out, so I decided to consolidate, in a separate section, additional professional advice from leaders in the field, particularly regarding suicide bereavement. All the information summarized here will have the author and book clearly identified so that therapists can go back to them if necessary.

After that, I will publish tips sent to me by the professionals I interviewed. I asked them to answer the following question: "What tip would you give a new therapist who is thinking about working with grief and suicide prevention and bereavement?" The reason why I did that was because I wanted to honor the time they set aside to help me with my research. My objective was to make sure all of them would be mentioned here, since I had a limited number of pages, which meant that I had to leave some of the interviews out.

1. William Worden, in *Grief Counseling and Grief Therapy*
How to facilitate uncomplicated grief:

- Help client actualize loss by talking about it, asking for details of service, etc. Visiting grave site can help.
- Revive memories of deceased, beginning with positive ones.
- If a client has experienced multiple losses, deal with them separately.
- Deal with affect or lack of it.
- Help identify and experience feelings.
  - Anger: may come from frustration or helplessness and is often directed at others. It may become depression when toward self. Look for suppressed anger.
  - Guilt: address it by reality-testing.
  - Anxiety/helplessness: help recognize how they managed it before the death. Keep in mind it may be related to death anxiety.
  - Sadness: assist in living without the deceased—for example, by introducing decision-making skills.
- Discourage life-changing decisions.
- Guide them toward finding meaning in loss; help reestablish a sense of control; facilitate emotional relocation of the deceased; provide time to grieve; normalize behavior; allow for individual differences, and examine defenses and coping styles.

How to tell children about death

- Take into account the child's cognitive capabilities and developmental stage. What cognitive concepts are needed to understand what happened? Inevitability, causality, finality, and irreversibility of death.

- Tell them what they need to know. Examples: that they will be cared for and that they didn't cause the death.
- Give them clear, simple information, such as causes and circumstances of death.
- Include them in some of the decisions; it's good for them to feel involved.
- Maintain daily routine.
- Make sure there is someone who can listen to their needs.
- Foster/allow them to find ways to remember the dead person, e.g., a memory book.

2. Pauline Sutcliffe, Guinevere Tufnell, and Ursula Cornish, in *Working with the Dying and Bereaved*

- When working with families, assess their configuration.
- Help with the reorganization of the family system and reinvestment in other relationships and life pursuits. Sometimes, families hold rigidly to old patterns.
- The main challenges for families are to share acknowledgment of reality and to share the experience of the loss.
- Don't isolate the kids; that impends the grief process. Children become more symptomatic when parents block grieving.
- Rituals are ways to confront death directly, opportunities to share grief and find comfort.
- Attend to difficult reactions so that they can be accepted by family members. Sometimes, one member is isolated or scapegoated, which shatters family cohesion.
- Avoid minimizing the loss.

- Take some aspects into consideration: the family's level of functioning, the sociocultural context, the prior role of the deceased, and the timing of loss in the family cycle.

3. Christopher Lukas and Henry Seiden, in *Silent Grief: Living in the Wake of Suicide*

How to approach children about suicide death:
- Don't leave them alone, because that adds to their confusion.
- Depending on their developmental age, children think their wishes come true, which may cause them to believe they are guilty for the suicide.
- Don't be silent about the suicide; it not only denies healing, but also obscures the real story.
- Be truthful, or they will create their own version of the death.
- Give them space to express their feelings; listen, fill in the gaps.
- Pay attention to non-verbal behavior; guess when necessary.
- Remember: children's thinking is concrete, with little abstraction. Think emotionally, because they will pick up your emotional tone.
- Wait for them to process the information;
- Keep the door open for tears and physical affection.

4. Kay Redfield Jamison, *in Night Falls Fast: Understanding Suicide*

How to approach children:

"The initial communication, or lack of communication, about the circumstances of a parent's death can be critical to a child's ability to accept and deal with suicide."

"It is important that children be told the truth as completely and quickly as they are able to take it in. Efforts to 'protect' or 'shield' a child almost invariably come back to haunt him or her by creating a web of distortions and misperceptions and a 'conspiracy of silence.'"

5. Charles Figley, Brian Bride and Nicholas Mazza, in *Death and Trauma: The Traumatology of Grieving*

When treating families:

- Assess: alliances and conflicts between dyads and triads; level of autonomy of individuals and subsystems; level of openness; clarity of boundaries; resources and social support; ethnic, religious and spiritual considerations.
- Help them see their competencies as individuals and subgroups (siblings, parents).
- View interactions as feedback loops. For example, a family with unresolved grief finds it circling back because there is no new information.

6. Patrick O'Malley and Tim Madigan, in *Getting Grief Right: Finding Your Story of Love in the Sorrow of Loss*

What not to say:

- Don't question the length and intensity of bereavement.
- Don't assume your experience is the same.
- Don't compliment mourners on their courage and strength, because it may cause them to hold back their feelings.
- Don't give advice; avoid clichés.

- Don't try to move them from one emotional place to another to make yourself more comfortable.

Finally, a detailed book on how to talk to children is worth mentioning as well—*Finding the Words*, by Dr. Alan Wolfelt. It goes into detailed examples of what can be said to children of specific ages. Due to the nature of the book, I will not produce this; there are simply too many helpful suggestions. I will only single out a paragraph that represents his overall approach:

"Children operate on a level of feelings and emotions first and logic second. There is a direct line between your feelings and her feelings. You send out signals about your emotions and your wellbeing. When she senses insincerity or falseness, she, in turn, feels insecure. To best companion, start with authenticity: be your true self, your highest self, your best self, and respond with love and respect to whatever questions she may have about death and dying."

TIPS FROM EXPERIENCED THERAPISTS

1. Keith Dempsey, counselor, chair of the department of the counseling program at George Fox University, Portland, Oregon.

When new counselors are working with grief, they often get nervous when clients mention the thought of suicide. Of course, this feels like a huge responsibility to ensure safety for the client. Such work can be overwhelming for even the most seasoned clinician. New clinicians must understand there is more reason to worry when clients are not talking about the grief and suicidal ideations they experience. Utilize this moment to be supportive, hear their story, and help work through the pain to go on.

2. Tracy Sandor, counselor.

It can be difficult to predict which clients' stories will impact you personally. Allow yourself to feel their pain, and to be with them emotionally. Then, allow time following the session to process its impact on you. Develop methods for releasing and expressing your emotions, and create rituals that are meaningful to you that support your efforts at letting go of others' pain. Prayer, meditation, yoga movements, and time with supportive colleagues are all necessary components of doing grief work for me.

3. Richard Shaw, counselor.

When working with clients around grief and loss issues, go toward the grief, go toward the pain. Spoken, processed pain and loss are always more powerful and healthy then unspoken, unprocessed grief and loss.

4. Giovana Kreuz, clinical psychologist in São Paulo, Brazil.

We can only invite people to talk if we are willing to listen

The lack of professional experience and technical skills, and the fear of accountability, can sometimes make us 'deaf' to the multitude of factors that place our clients in a place of no belonging, and of emotional homelessness. In many instances, they feel threatened because they can't find a safe place or a trusted person to talk to about their suicidal thoughts. It is with this in mind that I reflected on what to say to beginning therapists. The main issue at hand is how to clear the way of our listening so that we don't fall into the trap of self-protection.

There is no easy answer, but some aspects should be part of our professional journey: our own therapy and supervision, and an ongoing quest for learning. The ability to engage in a mindful connection with our patients is also key;

this includes tuning into their body language, and symbolic language, to attend to all our senses and, most importantly, our capacity to love. Yes, love! This is the only source of a safe place in the world. There is no chance of healing without it; love allows us to reach our patients and rescue their delicate and unique stories.

5. Georgena Eggleston, MA, RScP, CRS, trauma specialist/grief guide.

Imagine a horizontal figure eight, with your client in one loop and you in the other. Now scan YOUR body. Notice any tense, tight places or unusual sensations. Place you attention here without judgment.

What happens? Does the ache or pain evaporate? Breathe.

Now, take your cleared attention back to your client with the intention that you are meeting them free of worry, doubt, dread, or fear.

Breathe into the powerful presence that you are in this moment.

6. Karen Scavacini, clinical psychologist and CEO of the Vita Alere Institute of Prevention and Postvention, in São Paulo, Brazil.

The first time I facilitated a support group, I came back home crying and wondering, "Who am I to help these people? They need so much!" I felt powerless, with no technical skills for the task. But then I thought, "If it's painful for me, what about for them, who hold all that and have no one to talk to?" Since then, I've been working for years with suicidal patients and mourners. Sometimes, the pain is so dense I can practically touch it.

Hearing a parent talk about the loss of a child is overwhelming, but with time, compassion, training, and self-care, we become capable of embracing the hurt and transform it into love and hope, so that the lost person's life becomes more important than their death. To be a safe place in the midst of the tsunami that has invaded their lives is to believe that they can move forward and to show them that they are not alone. This makes all the difference.

References

1. American Foundation for Suicide Prevention suicide aftermath toolkit http://www.sprc.org/sites/default/files/resource-program/ AfteraSuicideToolkitforSchools.pdf

2. Bonanno, G. A., Field, N. P., Gal-Oz, E. (2003). Continuing bonds and adjustment at 5 years after the death of a spouse. Journal of Consulting and Clinical Psychology, 71, 110-117.

3. Bonanno, G. A. (2009). The other side of sadness: What the new science of bereavement tells us about life after loss. New York, NY: Basic books.
4. Boss, P. (1999). Ambiguous loss: Learning to live with unresolved grief. Cambridge, Massachusetts: Harvard University Press.

5. Cain, A. (1972). Survivors of suicide. Springfield, IL: Charles Thomas.

6. Cerel, J., Padgett, J. H., Conwell, Y., & Reed, G. A. (2009). A call for research: The need to better understand the impact of support groups for suicide survivors. Suicide and Life-Threatening Behavior, 39(3), 269–281. https://doi.org/10.1521/suli.2009.39.3.269

7. Cobain, B., & Larch, J. (2006). Dying to be free: A healing guide for families after a suicide. Center City, MI: Hazelden Publishing.

8. Cvinar, J. G. (2005). Do suicide survivors suffer social stigma: A review of the literature. Perspectives in Psychiatric Care, 41(1), 14–21. https://doi.org/10.1111/j.0031-5990.2005.00004.x

9. Danto, B. & Kutscher, A. H. (1977). Suicide and bereavement. New York, NY: MSS Information Corporation.
Eggleston, G. (2015). A new mourning: Discovering the gifts in grief. Bloomington, IN: Balboa Press.

10. Figley, C., Bride, B., & Mazza, N. (1997). Death and trauma: The traumatology of grieving. Washington, DC: Taylor & Francis.

11. Hemingway, M. (2015). "Out came the sun: Overcoming the legacy of mental illness, addiction, and suicide in my family. New York, NY: Regan Arts.

12. Inglis, K. (2018). Notes from the everlost: a field guide to grief. Boulder, CO: Shambhala.

13. Jamison, K. R. (1999). Night falls fast: Understanding suicide. New York, NY: Alfred A. Knopf.

14. Konigsberg, R. D. (2011). The truth about grief: The myth of its five stages and the new science of loss. New York, NY: Simon & Schuster.

15. Kübler-Ross, E., & Kessler, D. (1969). On death and dying: What the dying have to teach doctors, nurses, clergy and their own families. New York, NY: Collier Books.

16. Kübler-Ross, E. (1999). The tunnel and the light: essential insights on living and dying. New York, NY: Marlowe & Company.

17. Kübler-Ross, E., & Kessler, D. (2005). On grief and grieving: finding the meaning of grief through the five stages of loss. New York, NY: Scribner.

18. Lukas, C. & Seiden, H. (2007). Silent grief: living in the wake of suicide. London, UK: Jessica Kingsley Publishers.

19. Miller, A. (2006). The body never lies: The lingering effects of hurtful parenting. New York, NY: W.W. Norton & Company.

20. O'Malley, P. & Madign, T. (2017). Getting grief right: finding your story of love in the sorrow of loss. Boulder, CO: Sounds True.

21. O'Rourke, M. (2011). The long goodbye: A memoir. New York, NY: Riverhead Books.

22. Prigerson, H. G., Shear, M. K., Jacobs, S. C., Reynolds, C. F.,

Maciejewski, P. K., Davidson, J. R. (1999). Consensus criteria for traumatic grief. A preliminary empirical test. British Journal of Psychiatry, 174, 67–73.

23. Rosof, B. (1994). The worst loss: how families heal from the death of a child. New York, NY: Henry Holt and Company.

24. Ross, B. E. (1997). After suicide: A ray of hope for those left behind. Cambridge, MA: Perseus Publishing.

25. Samuel, J. (2017). Grief works: Stories of life, death, and surviving. New York, NY: Scribner.

26. Shneidman, E. (1977). "To the bereaved of a suicide" in Suicide and bereavement. New York, NY: MSS Information Corporation.

27. Smith, Tom (2013). The unique grief of suicide: questions & hope. Bloomington, IN: iUniverse.

28. Styron, W. (1992). Darkness visible: A memoir of madness. Knopf Doubleday Publishing Group.

29. Sutcliffe, P., Tufnell, G. & Cornish, U. (1998). Working with the dying and bereaved: systemic approaches to therapeutic work. New York, NY: Routledge. Van der Kolk, B. (2015). The body keeps the score: Brain, mind, and boy in the healing of trauma. New York, NY: Penguin Books.

30. Viorst, J. (1986) Necessary losses: The loves, illusions, dependencies, and impossible expectations that all of us have to give up in order to grow. New York, NY: The Free Press.

31. Wolfelt, A. (2013). Finding the words: How to talk with children and teens about death, suicide, funerals, homicide, cremation, and other end-

of-life matters. Fort Collins, CO: Companion Press.

32. Worden, J. W. (2009) (4th ed). Grief counseling and grief therapy: a handbook for the mental health practitioner. New York, NY: Springer.
33. Wright, H. N. (1995). Recovering from the losses of life. Grand Rapids, MN: Fleming H. Revell.

34. Yalom, I. (2017). Becoming myself. New York, NY: Basic Books.

35. Yalom, I. (2008). Staring at the sun: Overcoming the terror of death. San Francisco, CA: Jossey-Bass.

CHAPTER NINE

Youth and Suicide: A Worldwide Concern

Youth suicide rates have been growing over the years, which has led to several initiatives worldwide. According to WHO[1], in 2016, suicide was the second-leading cause of death within the 15-29 age group, losing only to road injury. In the United States, the CDC reported that the rate of voluntary death within the 15-24 age range for females jumped from 3.0 per 100,000 in 1999 to 5.8 in 2017. For males, it went from 16.8 in 1999 to 22.7 in 2017[2]. In 2017, the American Institute of Mental Health divulged that the prevalence of serious suicidal thoughts was highest among adults ages 18-25 (10.5 percent)[3].

When looking at the US data from 1975 to 2015 by gender, the 15-19 age group variations follow similar patterns for males and females, although males have rates that are more than double those of females[4]. Considering the broad range of factors involved in suicide, these numbers provide a good snapshot of how a single component can directly influence the numbers. From 2007 to 2015, largely after the 2008 economic crisis that affected millions of American families, female teen suicide reached its highest point since 1975, increasing from 2.4 to 5.1 per 100,000. For boys, it grew from 10.8 to 14.2. The crisis had long-lasting ramifications ranging from financial strain to family dissolution and socioeconomic migration.

In an article published in 2018, Johan Bilsen cited that approximately 50 percent of youth suicide is related to family factors[5], including family dynamics, communication patterns, neglect, violence, substance abuse, and history of mental disorders. When it comes to the latter, he clarifies:

"It is not clear whether these disorders directly influence the suicidal behavior of the child, or rather do so indirectly, through mental disorders evoked in the child as a result of this family context."

The author mentions that suicidal behavior of family members has also been linked to youth suicide. This is a hot topic of discussion in the field, because the mechanisms behind it are still unclear. In some cases, youngsters may harm themselves as a result of imitation. Genetics may also play a role. Twin studies have shown a higher risk for those with a biological family history of self-inflicted death, even in kids who were adopted, which signals the impact of genetics. The association with parental divorce is weak and might be more closely related to the life changes provoked by it, such as financial difficulties, relational factors, and the implications of living in a single-parent family.

Young people are more vulnerable to mental health problems, particularly in adolescence, when they go through changes as they search for their own identity. Mood swings and heightened emotions are normal traits of adolescence. These are part of the individual's search for self, as well as a natural response to increased responsibilities. Brain development also plays a significant part in behavior during this phase.

In the teenage years, the midbrain, where emotions are processed, is well-developed, while the formation of the connections of the prefrontal cortex, responsible for reasoning, are still underway. It is this area that allows us to plan, moderate social behavior, prioritize, and think logically. As a result, adolescents are prone to misinterpret social cues, act on impulse, and engage in risky behavior. This is where suicidal ideation may come into play.

It is in adolescence that we make decisions about the future, start having intimate relationships, get in touch with our own values and beliefs, and build independence, to mention just a few aspects. All this happens while experiencing profound psychological and physical changes.

Social media

Since the launch of the smartphone in 2007, internet access has become an essential part of most people's lives, and the use of social media has recently risen to unprecedented popularity. There is no doubt that establishing connections online is not necessarily negative. Quite the contrary—the benefits for the youth are many. It enables them to improve communication skills, to broaden their social network, and to develop new interests. The problems arise when the online environment substitutes for real-life relationships and activities, when it highjacks a per-son's capacity to look outside their screens and find joy elsewhere.

The correlation between mental health and screen time has been the subject of an increasing number of recent studies, and the results paint a somber picture. In the United Kingdom, the Royal Society for Public Health published a report[6] on the impact of social media and young people's mental health and wellbeing.

The study found that 91 percent of 16-24-year-olds use the internet for social networking, which is linked with higher rates of anxiety, depression, and poor sleep. It has been described as more addictive than cigarettes and alcohol. Bullying was experienced by 70 percent of the respondents. The same rate was found when it came to the rise of anxiety and depression within this age group.

One of the aspects investigated was the new concept of 'Fear of Missing Out' (FoMO), a phrase commonly used by young people and a concept closely associated with anxiety. It consists of the worry that if you are not connected, you will be missing out on joyful activities as they happen. This leads to the constant need to recheck messages and posts online. According to the study, FoMO is also linked with lower mood and lower life satisfaction.

The UK research tried to measure how 1,479 people aged 16-24 felt they were impacted by the five most popular social media platforms: Instagram, Facebook, Snapchat, Twitter, and YouTube. The questions explored themes such as sleep, loneliness, emotional support, access to health information, body image, self-expression, community building, and real-world relationships. YouTube led with the most positive results, followed by Twitter, Facebook, and Snapchat. Instagram, which consists entirely of images and videos, was found to have the most negative impact.

Daily internet usage has increased dramatically in the UK, jumping from 35 percent of the population in 2006 to 82 percent in 2016. Social media usage has seen similar growth. In 2007, only 22 percent of people had at least one profile; by 2016, the percentage had risen to 89 percent. The most popular platforms are Facebook, with around thirty million UK users, and Twitter, with fifteen million, followed by the then existent Google+, LinkedIn, Pinterest, Instagram, and Snapchat.

In the United States, the statistics are equally disquieting. A 2017 study[7] conducted with 506,820 youngsters between the ages of 13-18 found that adolescents who spent more screen time had a significantly higher likelihood to experience depressive symptoms or have at least one suicide-related outcome. The suicide rate increase was more prominent in females, growing 65 percent between 2010 and 2015, from 2.93 to 4.21 per 100,000. It more than doubled from the late 1990s to 2015 (1.99 to 4.21).

As mentioned before, finding a balance between life on and off the screen is crucial. The US study found that adolescents using electronic devices three or more hours daily had 34-percent more chance of having at least one suicide-related outcome than those using devices two or fewer hours a day. When visiting social media sites every day, teenagers were 13 percent more likely to report high levels of depressive symptoms than those who used them less often.

According to the authors of the study, one of the factors that contribute to depression is the many popularity measures created by Facebook, which may lead to feelings of inadequacy when a young person sees their 'friend' having a good time. The researchers observe, however, that this is not true for all users. If well-adjusted, the effect may be the opposite: a boost in the adolescent's positive feelings about themselves.

When looking at the numbers in the US, social media reaches the vast majority of the population, particularly the youth. According to a Pew Research Center 2019 survey[8], 90 percent of individuals in the 18-24 age group have a habit of checking videos on YouTube. In second place comes Facebook, with 76 percent, then Instagram, being mentioned by 75 percent, Snapchat, with 73 percent, and Twitter with 44 percent.

The frequency also gives us an idea of how much time this age group spends checking posts, videos, and pictures online. Facebook is visited daily by 74 percent of 18-24-year-olds, Instagram by 63 percent, Snapchat by 61 percent, YouTube by 51 percent, and Twitter by 42 percent. The survey asked the participants if they checked these platforms several times a day. For Facebook, 51 percent answered 'yes,' followed by Snapchat, with 46 percent, Instagram with 42 percent, YouTube with 32 percent, and Twitter with 25 percent. Note that all this data doesn't account for the hours spent messaging on other platforms.

When being online can be deadly

One of the most distressing experiences I had when writing this book was when I contacted an online forum after being notified that the participants were stimulating youngsters to kill themselves. Engaging with them was very easy. Before I chatted with anyone, I checked their Frequently Asked Questions (FAQ), which directly informed the reader about their beliefs regarding self-inflicted death:

"Our view is that suicide should be a right for all, except for children and adults who are unable to take responsibility for their actions."

The forum works like this: first-time users are greeted with the phrase, "Welcome, we're sorry you're here." Then, they can register and leave a message, which can be read by all the members. From then on, the interaction is restricted between the new user, who leaves an email address, and those who respond to the message.

The main idea of the group is to allow the theme to be discussed openly and without judgment, allowing the person to feel at ease exposing their feelings and what they are going through. If the user is determined to die, the members will help them forward:

"Whenever one of our members dies by suicide, we understand that it was probably the best option for this person. We respect their decision, and we were happy that they finally escaped their pain."

When I wrote to them, I introduced myself as a sixteen-year-old girl named Nina. The story I created was that my parents were distant and traveled six days a week. I felt lonely and had no intention to go on living. I told them that I had already tried to kill myself twice before, one of those times using gas inhalation, and I certainly did not want to 'fail' again. The post was straightforward: next time, I would use my father's gun, since I had heard that the most effective way would be a shot to the back of the head. Finally, I asked someone to give me guidance.

On the same day, I received three messages. In one of them, a man theoretically named Robert advised me not to kill myself. He sent me his email in case I needed to talk. The second had the same tone—this time, a woman who didn't mention her name. The third message was from a thirty-something Minneapolis nurse, who replied:

"PLEASE do not try to shoot on the back or any other area of the head. I work in the emergency sector of a hospital and I'm tired of seeing poor souls who do this and end up here alive but with serious brain injuries. If you really want to die, and hopefully you don't, hanging yourself is a much more reliable and effective method. This is the method that I will use myself, so I know about the subject. If you need to talk about this, send me an email. Take care, Cami."

After the first email was exchanged, we started chatting. Cami told me that she had tried suicide three times without 'success,' so she devoted herself to studying different methods of doing it without pain and with the certainty that she would complete the suicide next time.

Although she introduced herself as someone who liked to help others, I felt that there was something wrong with her tone and demeanor. My first suspicion was that although she made herself available to listen to what I had to say, including my ambivalence about killing myself, she was always quick to change the subject to asphyxiation, so her interest was clearly to stimulate my death and not to avoid it.

During our conversations, I made several inquiries about her conviction that she would take her own life at some point. If she was so sure of that and had studied the methods deeply, what kept her from doing it? The answers were evasive and unconvincing, things like "the time has not come yet." She even mentioned that she once "tested" the hanging for twelve seconds and had almost lost consciousness.

She also asked repeatedly if I had a webcam, ensuring that her intention was just to make sure I would tie the knot properly. She even sent me an email with a website that taught how to tie knots, pointing out what kind I should use so they wouldn't come undone during the process.

Interested to see how far she would go, I proposed to her that we do it together. Cami accepted on the spot, thanking me for my suggestion, and we arranged to do it three days later. The last contact I had with Cami was when we set the time and day to perform the combined suicide. On the arranged day, I arrived home late and saw many emails from her, questioning if I had changed my mind. I deleted them all and blocked her. My research was done.

During the days I exchanged messages with Cami, I initiated contact with Robert, the man who'd tried to dissuade me. I was honest with him by revealing I was a journalist doing research for a suicide book. At first, he was furious that I had lied, but soon he understood and agreed to give me an interview by email.

We kept in touch for a week. He said he always visited the group looking for young people (according to him, most visitors were between sixteen and twenty-one years of age) with the intention of helping them to see other options in life. Robert was blind in one eye and was wheelchair-bound, so he had already experienced a heavy amount of suffering, yet he seemed to have a positive and optimistic outlook on life.

Over time, he became obsessive in his emails, accusing me of "not being his friend as he thought." He wanted to chat every day and left numerous email messages demanding immediate reply. The short-lived immersion I made in such a forum was enough to identify the profile of two people with opposing but equally unhealthy intentions and goals in their approach to others. Robert was also blocked from my contact list.

Rising rates in college students

The American College Health Association[9], ACHA, published its Spring 2018 student health assessment, which had 88,178 participants. The report collects data about students' behavior, habits, and perceptions on a variety of topics. One of the sections asks respondents to cite the main medical problems they experienced within the previous twelve months. Psychiatric conditions were cited by 9.2 percent of them, not including Attention Deficit and Hyperactivity Disorder, ADHD, which was mentioned by an additional 7.8 percent.

The survey asked students to identify which factors had negatively affected their academic performance. Stress was placed at the top of the list with 33.2 percent, followed by anxiety (26.5 percent), sleep difficulties (21.8 percent), and depression (18.7 percent), all of which have a direct impact on mental health. Many do not seek help.

The data shows a concerning number of youngsters who need professional attention and support from their family and peers, but most people feel that they wouldn't be equipped to take action. Knowing how to approach this population can make a difference in the manner in which they will respond, so I have gathered here some basic tips from books I've read and other credible sources.

Watch for

- Academic problems: lack of interest, sudden drop in grades, skipping class, difficulty concentrating, and aggression toward teachers and student peers.
- Behavioral changes: withdrawal, disregard for personal appearance, substance use (or increase of it), mood swings, risk-taking activities, self-harm/self-mutilation (mainly cutting), and eating changes.
- Speech: discussion of death and related themes, such as pain, suicide, and despair.

What helps

- Relationships are the most important asset. Stay close, offer non-judgmental help, and as much as possible (with consent), involve family, friends, teachers, faculty, or staff. Build an empathic community.
- Healthy habits: adequate sleep, diet, physical exercise, health care, and counseling. Most colleges have mental health services for their students.
- If you are a parent, stay involved in their academic life. If you have kids who are still in school, attend events that are relevant to them, such as dance performances and sports matches. If there are academic problems, talk to teachers and faculty. If they are in college, which many times means that they are out of state, connect with them by calling, texting, and video chatting. What they need to know is that you care. This is particularly important for freshmen, because they are going through many adaptations,

so they need to feel that family support is still there.

- When talking to your kid, avoid "right or wrong" comments. Ask open-ended questions (those that are not answered by a simple yes or no). This helps them open up to you. Listen, listen, listen. Many times, what they need is to be heard, not necessarily to be given specific advice. Kids usually make it clear when they want your objective guidance. A good approach is to relate their problems to similar ones that you have had in the past. This is less intrusive than saying things like, "I think you should" Give them space to figure out what is best for them.

- Whenever it's possible, and this depends on consent and your kid's age, monitor their online activities. Set time limits. Using the internet is not a problem per se—much to the contrary, it is essential for their academic and social development. Using too much of it or substituting human contact by social media, however, is what raises concern.

Self-harm in adolescence

When I published the first edition of this book, in 2008, self-harm was not a central issue when it came to suicide, but the scenario has changed dramatically over the last few years. Researchers around the world are trying to find the long-term psychological consequences it may have on individuals and its relationship with self-inflicted death. Part of the reason why the scientific community still struggles to aggregate reliable data about self-harm is due to the fact that researchers are still discussing the standard terms for it. This has a direct impact on variations of estimates across the globe. Some of the interchangeable definitions used are self-injury, DSH, self-mutilation, parasuicide, and attempted suicide.

In 2018, the Journal of the American Academy of Child and Adolescent Psychiatry[10] published a large study on the matter. The authors analyzed 172 datasets of reported self-harm (1990-2015) in 597,548 adolescent participants from forty-one countries. Here are some of their conclusions:

- The lifetime prevalence of self-harm was 16.9 percent with an increase in 2015.
- Girls are more likely to hurt themselves.
- Teens start on average at age thirteen (47 percent report 1 or 2 episodes, 21.7 percent 3 to 5 incidents, 21.6 percent 6 to 10, and 5 percent more than 10).
- The most common type of self-harm is cutting (45 percent), followed by preventing wounds from healing (33 percent), headbanging (31 percent), biting (29 percent), and scratching (28 percent).
- The most frequent reason for self-harm is to obtain relief from thoughts or feelings.
- Slightly more than half sought help, mostly from friends.
- Self-harm is associated with higher risks of suicidal ideation and attempts, particularly for those who do it frequently.

Another interesting Australian study looked at the long-term psychosocial outcomes associated with self-harm during the teenage years. The research started in 1992 and ended in 2014, with 1,943 adolescents participating from forty-four schools across the state of Victoria. They concluded that those who self-harmed when young were more likely to experience a wide range of psychosocial problems later in life, such as depression, anxiety, substance use, and social disadvantages, including divorce and financial hardship.

Marcelo (pseudonym) is a good example of such a correlation. When I interviewed him in July 2019, he was forty-five years old and had just separated from his wife, which led him to a suicide attempt, the fourth of his life. As a child, at the age of six, he was sexually abused by a neighbor for more than a year:

"He used to abuse and threaten us (three friends) with violence. We were constantly scared to play outside because of him. I never told my parents."

After the abuse, he started to hurt himself by banging his head on the wall. One day, when he was twelve years old, Marcelo saw the abuser riding his bike outside his house and decided to kill him. He went home, grabbed his father's gun, stepped outside, and shot the young man twice, missing him both times. A few months later, for the first time, he attempted suicide by covering himself with a blanket and lying on the street. He believed that the blanket would hide him from drivers. He was rescued by neighbors.

Fortunately, soon after the incident, his family moved to another area of town. He was finally free of his abuser, but the psychological pain and its impacts remained. Between the ages of twelve and fourteen, Marcelo tried to kill himself twice by hanging, once by pulling a cord wrapped around his neck (which made him lose consciousness), and then once by tying the cord to a tree. The branch was not strong enough, so he fell to the ground. He remembers trying to hurt himself in many different ways. "I would touch electric wires and think, 'If I get a shock, so be it.' At thirteen, I started to drink."

As a young adult, he engaged in several high-risk activities, getting injured quite constantly, and using alcohol as a means to numb the pain. Any kind of conflict or aggression would make him shut down and isolate himself. Romantic relationships were hard to come by, because he would not let anyone touch him. "I have to do it first, otherwise, it overwhelms

me. It is as if something in my brain interprets touch as a threat."
At the age of forty-two, his marriage came to an end. After another
suicide attempt, and still never having told anyone about his abuse,
Marcelo sought help. It was during therapy that he finally understood the
correlation between his shattered childhood and his interpersonal reactions to the trauma.

*"I learned to identify and avoid external triggers. I can't see images of
blood or any extreme violence, even on TV. Children in distress, particularly crying,
or adults yelling are also too much for me. Understanding my own traumas has
made me quite attuned to kids' behaviors. When I see that a child is overreacting
to something and I recognize that their reaction is odd, I try to warn the parents so
that they can pay attention to them."*

Marcelo has never told his parents or his ex-wife about what happened
to him. Apart from his therapist, the only person who knows is his
half-sister, who became aware of his ordeal a few months before our
interview. This may seem unusual, but the reality is that silence and
shame are still the hallmarks of traumatic experiences. Judith Herman,
professor of psychiatry at Harvard Medical School, reminds us of that
in her book, *Trauma and Recovery: The Aftermath of Violence—From Domestic
Abuse to Political Terror*[1]:

*"The conflict between the will to deny horrible events and the will to
proclaim them aloud is the central dialectic of psychological trauma. People who
have survived atrocities often tell their stories in a highly emotional, contradictory,
and fragmented manner that undermines their credibility and thereby serves the
twin imperatives of truth-telling and secrecy. When the truth is finally recognized,
survivors can begin their recovery. But far too often secrecy prevails, and the story of
the traumatic event surfaces not as a verbal narrative but as a symptom."*

Non-Suicidal Self-Injury (NSSI)

Jennifer Muehlenkamp, professor of psychology at the University of Wisconsin, Eau Claire, is a specialist in NSSI, which is defined as "behaviors in which an individual intentionally harms the body without overt suicidal intent." In other words, the intent to die is not present. These individuals resort to harming themselves in order to get relief from emotional pain, and to distract or escape from stressful situations.

Together with colleagues, she surveyed 14,372 American college students, in order to identify severity, main practices, prevalence, perceived dependency, and help-seeking. They found that an average of 15.3 percent of students had previously engaged in NSSI. Females had a higher probability to self-injure when they were upset or needed attention. Males reported anger as the main drive, as well as the presence of intoxication. More than half had disclosed their NSSI, but less than 9 percent had done so to a mental health professional.

In a 2013 study, Jennifer and colleagues surveyed 1,243 college students, searching for their perceived social support and disclosure experiences. They had an average of twenty-one years of age and were mostly Caucasian. Approximately 15 percent endorsed NSSI. When I interviewed Jennifer on Skype, she highlighted the fact that individuals with repetitive NSSI had significantly lower perceived social support from family members, and fewer people to seek advice from. It was surprising to me to learn that support groups are not recommended for treating this population:

"The clinical recommendation is that groups that focus on self-injury or that are designed to be comprised mostly of individuals who self-injure, especially teenagers, are not recommended because of the contagion that happens. There can be a sense of competition by sharing strategies, for instance. Discussion and support groups are not indicated. Treatment should focus on strengthening interpersonal

bonds alongside emotion regulation. Improving responses to disclosures of NSSI is needed to promote communication about this behavior and the perceived helpfulness of such conversations."

The authors of the article found higher suicidal behavior in this population when compared to those who never engaged in NSSI, which is in agreement with other studies. As for what motivated these young adults, she cited difficulty coping with emotional distress, particularly self-hate, and elements linked to distress in interpersonal relationships and difficulties in building friendships and communication, as well as in solving conflicts, anger, and anxiety. Jennifer mentioned that teenagers are at higher risk, particularly due to the biological changes they experience and the need to figure out who they are. The peak ages for this behavior are from thirteen to seventeen. To illustrate the intensity of feelings typical of young adults, she told me of a patient who, after an argument with a girlfriend, cut herself:

> *"She was no good, nobody would love her, nobody had ever loved her. She was angry, anxious that she wouldn't get the relationship back, guilty about the harsh things that she had said to her girlfriend. She tried to text and call her with no success. Finally, the girlfriend called her and told her to leave her alone. My client got even more upset. She thought she had lost the relationship. It snow-balled into 'none of my friends like me, I don't fit anywhere,' so the urges to self-injure intensified. She started to blame herself for being generally a horrible person. She went into her bedroom where she had instruments for her self-injuring, pulled them out, and injured herself."*

According to Jennifer, 25 percent of people who engage in NSSI go on to attempt suicide in the future. If you reverse this datapoint, research shows that within those who attempted suicide, 50 percent to 90 percent report a history of self-injury. As for protective factors, she mentioned involving the family in the treatment of NSSI:

"Adolescents who have a stronger connection with at least one primary caregiver are more protected against self-injury. If they do engage in it, it is less severe. If they see a therapist, they recover more quickly."

I asked Jennifer about warning signs, and she told me that although self-injury can be hard to detect, some changes in behavior may help identify it. For example, some indicators include if the child is spending more time alone or in the bathroom, or if they are wearing clothing that covers up key aspects of their body, such as their forearms and upper thighs, which are the most predominant places for cutting and burning:

"In the summer, when it's warm out, notice if your child is wearing either a lot of bracelets and jewelry or longer sleeves, longer skirts and pants than normal. Certainly, if they are hanging out with kids whom you know self-injure, you want to ask them about it, because the affiliation can be there. Watch for signs of the use of bandages or first-aid to deal with wounds. Those might show up in garbage bins. This practice is pretty secret, and they get creative to keep it secret."

Other aspects of self-harm:

- The first episode commonly occurs between the ages of twelve and sixteen, dropping in frequency until at least the end of the twenties.
- The risk of suicide is highest in the first six months after an episode of self-harm.
- It is associated with a higher risk of accidental death or permanent disability.
- Emotional functions of self-harm are the self-punishment, anger expression, tension relief, a distraction from an intolerable situation, and assertion of autonomy.
- Studies in high-income countries consistently report a prevalence

of approximately 10 percent among young people.

In 2018, the World Federation for Mental Health published the report, *Young People and Mental Health in a Changing World*[12]. In it, they highlighted the main factors related to self-harm:

Demographic Factors

Age <20 years

Female gender

Low socioeconomic status

Low level of education Divorced/separated

LGBTQ+

Criminal record

Childhood sexual assault

Physical assault victimization

Psychiatric Factors

Depression

Substance abuse

Previous psychiatric hospitalization

Personality disorders

Anxiety disorder

Psychological Factors

High impulsivity

Poor problem-solving skills

Hopelessness

Low self-esteem

Perfectionism

Self-criticism

Situational Factors

Current adverse life events

Intoxication

Social Factors

Lesbian, gay, bisexual, transgender, intersex

Adverse childhood experiences

Social isolation

Bullying victimization

Exposure to self-harm

Alcohol use

Onset of sexual activity

Loneliness

References

[1] https://www.who.int/mental_health/prevention/suicide/suicideprevent/en/

[2] https://www.cdc.gov/nchs/products/databriefs/db330.htm

[3] https://www.nimh.nih.gov/health/statistics/suicide.shtml

[4] https://www.cdc.gov/mmwr/volumes/66/wr/mm6630a6.htm

[5] https://www.ncbi.nlm.nih.gov/pmc/articles/PMC6218408/#B24

[6] https://www.rsph.org.uk/our-work/campaigns/status-of-mind.html

[7] Twenge, J. M., Joiner, T. E., Rogers, M. L., & Martin, G. N. (2018). Increases in Depressive Symptoms, Suicide-Related Outcomes, and Suicide Rates Among U.S. Adolescents After 2010 and Links to Increased New Media Screen Time. Clinical Psychological Science, 6(1), 3–17. https://doi.org/10.1177/2167702617723376

[8] https://www.pewresearch.org/fact-tank/2019/04/10/share-of-u-s-adults-using-social-media-including-facebook-is-mostly-unchanged-since-2018/

[9] https://www.acha.org/documents/ncha/NCHA-II_Spring_2018_

Reference_Group_Executive_Summary.pdf

[10] Gillies, et al. (2018). Prevalence and Characteristics of Self-Harm in

Adolescents: Meta-Analyses of Community-Based Studies 1990–2015.

Journal of American Academy of Child and Adolescent Psychia-try,

57(10), 732-741.

[11]Herman, J. (1997). Trauma and Recovery: The Aftermath of

Violence—From Domestic Abuse to Political Terror :   New York, NY:

Basic Books.

[12] https://wfmh.global/wp-content/uploads/WMHD_

REPORT_19_9_2018_FINAL.pdf

Paula Fontenelle

www.understandsuicide.com

Jabuti

FINALIST OF THEBRAZILIAN NATIONAL BOOK PRIZE